House Fires

Also by **Connor Franta**

Note to Self

A Work in Progress

House Fires

Written by Connor Franta

ATRIA BOOKS

New York   London   Toronto   Sydney   New Delhi

ATRIA
B O O K S

An Imprint of Simon & Schuster, Inc.
1230 Avenue of the Americas
New York, NY 10020

Note to readers: Some names and identifying details have been changed.

First Atria Books hardcover edition October 2021

ATRIA B O O K S and colophon are trademarks of Simon & Schuster, Inc.

For information about special discounts for bulk purchases, please contact Simon & Schuster Special Sales at 1-866-506-1949 or business@simonandschuster.com.

The Simon & Schuster Speakers Bureau can bring authors to your live event. For more information or to book an event, contact the Simon & Schuster Speakers Bureau at 1-866-248-3049 or visit our website at www.simonspeakers.com.

Interior design by Dana Sloan

Manufactured in the United States of America

1 3 5 7 9 10 8 6 4 2

Library of Congress Cataloging-in-Publication Data has been applied for.

ISBN 978-1-9821-7771-3
ISBN 978-1-9821-7773-7 (ebook)

Words for your Future

Contents

Contents

Contents

Contents

Contents

* The following pages contain depictions of depression, anxiety, suicidal thoughts, sexual assault, and other written topics, which some readers may find disturbing.

Time is a series of house fires. We're engulfed

in the heat of yesterday and passion transports

us to a heavenly state of mind. Blueprints in the

making. We're an eternity of nuance.

All our lives we float through success and

under failure, but need we not forget,

every ending hones a new beginning.

Everything is as it will be, but we are much

greater than who we once were. All the daily

burdens can be good fortune in disguise.

We blaze and burn and are taken to the ground,

but watch as we flourish better all over again.

Introduction

I've always felt a level of mental displacement and physical dysphoria in my brief existence in this world. Things are never fully right, and when they are, they rarely maintain a sense of ease, stability, or remain situated in their permanent, or perceived to be, places, and I've frequently fought the notion the world could so easily be black and white. It's complex and so are we. I'm reminded time and time again: Just because things are bad sometimes doesn't mean they will be that way forever. And, likewise, just because happy moments don't bolster endless effervescence doesn't mean you can't enjoy them while you embrace them in your arms.

This perpetual struggle, however, has fueled a growing anxiety over time. Like a shadowy creature, it wraps a set of thin, bony hands around my life's throat—even when I'm not fully aware of it—gripping silently and slowly until a smoky vignette closes in around me, until I'm engulfed in darkness. Or, taking a "glass half-full" perspective, this general sense of (sometimes sweat-inducing) curiosity

1

has led me to question seemingly all of the day's wonders—from if God's classification of "him" was a creation by men to hang a forgoing power over women since the very beginning of time, to why the fuck are eggs mainly classified as a breakfast food when they're clearly delicious enough to not remain exclusive to morning meals?

Who wrote all these rules? I have notes and just want to talk!

There are millions of potential algorithms that lead to why we are the way we are, how we become the people eventually we become, and although I think we'll ultimately never pinpoint one singular cause, I won't allow it to halt my search for today's many hidden answers.

Life's wildly too short to blindly accept all the automated responses, and it's too complex to believe in singular outcomes. There are seven billion people in this world and 52,850 light-years of galaxy around us. I refuse to believe we actually fully know anything at all. Our current understanding is that of a star amongst an ocean of nebulas. Our mere existence is malleable, so why not push the shapes our perspectives can take?

Why would anyone choose a sphere after discovering a great icosahedron exists? The search is where the fruit lies, and for me, it's always sweetest after the long haul. Come now, let's forage for nectarines.

In my first book, *A Work in Progress*, I reflected on the past—sliding across the surface of general details and simple stories from my youngest of years; offering a loving glimpse into Midwestern childhood whimsy and closeted teenage fantasy; stumbling into good fortune—and all the little pieces of how I'm putting together the puzzle that is myself.

In my second book, *Note to Self*, I released the painful truths of my then present, allowing those secrets to scream validity out of their void, and explored complex feelings rooted in sorrow dripping from a broken heart: the weight of wandering aimlessly into adulthood, the terror of wanting to take my own life, and the less written joys of dancing in the warm, euphoric unknown that comes from being free to be careless.

In this book, *House Fires*, I would like to question the increasing severity of the human experience in these modern times; the clarity that comes with transitioning away from childhood and into adulthood; the struggles, triumphs, confusion, magic, exhaustion, liberation, and all that lies in between. From camaraderie to sex to religion to casualty to identity to enlightenment, and beyond, this book explores all the lesser discussed facets of humanity in pursuit of nuanced vulnerability—an open examination of yesterday's corners and tomorrow's cosmos. These pages depict an autopsy of all my emotions.

For those who have followed along since the beginning, you're in for a real cherry on top of this trilogy sundae. If you are joining here as a first-time reader, that's wonderful too. You don't need to know the past to bask in the honest present, so this collection of writing is also wholeheartedly for you. Plus, the previous book is very very sad, and I don't want to put anyone through that depiction of heartache again. Well, you may cry here too, so don't drop your guard yet.

Your teens and your twenties are an eternal journey around the Talladega Superspeedway, and my jaw drops as I accelerate around every corner. I'm on my way out of the described "most influential time in a person's life," and although it remains uneasy, it's one hell of a nonsensical journey, and I'm honored to take part in it. Just when I think I have an aspect of it locked down—whether it be finance, routine, friendship, purpose, or romance—I peek over a new ledge and drop down, hurtling into a triple loop-de-loop spiral and humbled by another wobbled landing.

Things rarely remain serene. Things never seem to maintain the same. Just when you get a grip on one page of your existence, the next slips through your fingers, and it honestly seems like that cycle will continue forever. How PEACHY is that? Right sometimes. Wrong all the others.

Truth, and it's the last thing most people want to read about, is: I'm happy most of the time nowadays. I've finally located a balance in these tornado times, but it wasn't without effort or practice, and who knows how long it will last. But, all I know is I'm here right now and I couldn't smile bigger writing those words.

Over the past three years, I've been marinating in the young adulthood experience and I have a lot to say. Whether it be love, drugs, sex, religion, euphoria, trauma, triumph, heaven, or hell, it's all in here. And this, what you're reading, is everything I have now. All of it. This is brutal vulnerability in its rawest form, and similar to before, my words are wildly imperfect at times, but they are real and come directly from my heart of hearts, so I only ask that you open yours and take an interstellar dip with me into the chaos. My horizons are panoramic, and these perspectives have never been this crystal. And trust my words here, I am very well aware: Just because things are peaceful here in my present doesn't mean they were always this way, and it sure as hell doesn't properly convey the tall fires I walked through to arrive at this doorstep.

Adolescence is bliss and adulthood can be brutal, but the in-between is where the two intertwine in madness and in love.

This house may not yet be home, and many others have burned to the ground wrapped in warm fire along the way, but oh, I'll gladly dance in purgatory from sunup to sundown. You can count on it.

Chapter One

A Room Full of Mirrors

I t's an odd time to be queer because a future is no longer a luxury. The other day I realized how the fog surrounding the years in front of me formed there in the first place. It was an early morning amidst a California autumn (much warmer than you may think, and honestly, warmer than I'd like it to be). After putting away last night's clean dishes, warming up a kettle of water, and downing the tart coffee that followed, I pulled on my running apparel and was off to the streets for an unwinding sixty minutes of energy-induced endorphins. Bliss. Usually during my daily sunrise escapes, I entertain my mind by allowing it to wander, ponder, and get lost freely in a thought train. Today's staggeringly prolific topic (for me, at least) dawned on me while moving through one of America's queer arteries, the aorta if you will: West Hollywood, known for its rainbow sidewalks, thunderous drag queens, overpriced vodka sodas, relocated assemblage of twink clones, and the most visible male midriffs you'll ever spot in a single metropolitan area.

Rounding the corner somewhere between Sunset and Santa Monica, speeding past several versions of the humans just described, I began to wonder out of seemingly nowhere: Have I ever properly seen what lies in the future? And does it simmer down to the fact that millions of LGBTQIA+ people just like me never made it to a destination much farther than where I'm at now, for a multitude of reasons? Before the twenty-first century, queer people were never given the chance to properly eat the fruits of their days due to violence, persecution, disease, bigotry, hatred, and general careless abandonment pouring in from all directions. Not a single chance. At the time, most were set up to be let down as soon as they spoke their truth, and for those who did voice their opinions, many were blatantly ignored and left unaided by higher governmental powers during the AIDS crisis in the eighties and nineties. Many, of course, evaded the horrors and survived the unimaginable pain of those decades, but they are few and far between when compared to their heterosexual coupled counterparts who exist without question.

It wasn't until very recently that LGBTQIA+ people have even been given the chance to live a "normal" life. If you were privileged enough to come out as a teenager in the recent years of the twenty-first century, fall into the open arms of familial acceptance, and live in a geographical location where you didn't face persecution, you must realize: This has never happened. EVER. In all of human history. You are trailblazing an era of hope and freedom. And, because I fall into most of those unparalleled categories of pure fortune, I now know why it's been nearly impossible for me to picture my future: It's almost never been done before. Or, at the very least, it's incredibly scarce, and that uniqueness must be acknowledged.

There are barely any living examples existing in my personal life's blueprint to show me the way to tomorrow; no gentleman to invite me over to his home, introduce me to his husband, dog, adopted children, tell me about his twenty-year professorship at the nearby university, babble on about just having paid off his heavy student loans, cook an impressive meal he's too modest to fully boast about, whisper about current celebrity gossip, etc. A person to offer me an impressive array of beverages, snacks, and life's little luxuries along the way to their den or sitting room (oh wow, imagine a gay sitting room . . . chic as fuck), thus sharing with me a little something otherwise known as Gay Adulthood. I'm obviously stretching across many stereotypes here, but this is a heavy topic and I don't want to bring you down into a dark basement already, all right? There are plenty of opportunities to do that with my own life's musings let alone a fictional burgundy-cash-mere-cardigan-wearing man with a well-mannered silver-haired companion who goes exclusively by Christoph. Not Chris. Not Christian. Not Christopher. CHRISTOPH! Behind every lined jacket is sewn a golden thread of the truth—guys, gals, and nonbinary pals. Or, at the very least, in modern, urban, queer North America, the potential for validity is strong in this one. Champagne? Purified lemon-mint water? Gah, God love you. Okay, I'll stop with the clichéd lunacy. Let's proceed.

Now I've officially gone off the rails and onto the laughably fic-titious gravel road. I'm kidding. Don't mindfully roast me. Anyways, I do know that older queer people obviously exist in today's timeline (I've met them in all their beautiful shapes and sizes), but there aren't as many of them as there could be. They don't exist in the quantity that should have been. Millions of potential futures were lost during a gruesome and downright shameful period in global history. It's not like HIV/AIDS had an easy cure to be swiftly developed, but absolutely NOTHING was done for a struggling community and that's unspeakably insidious. For the ones who did live through this tragedy, they continued on through an unimaginably heavy period of persecution. My struggles with being out, loud, and proud are a sliver amongst their forest. Only years ago, it was universally dangerous, and like in countless countries around the world today, even, completely illegal. Regardless, I'm coming from a good, curious, yet confused place here, so allow me to work through this with you knowing that I may make a few mistakes.

It's become increasingly more difficult to picture me in a life like that of my parents—a married couple of thirty-five years with four children living peacefully in a small Midwestern town. Now, this could be a sign of the times, a direct result of my unprecedented career path, this gay conundrum I've proposed, or countless other impossible factors that will no doubt send me into a panicky spiral. WE DON'T NEEED TO GO THERE, yet. Do you remember the origami paper fortune-telling contraptions you used to make as kids? You'd take a sheet of 11- by 8.5-inch computer paper, fold it into various triangles, while writing various vague life questions on each flap, then you'd proceed to add numbers, colors, a new fold, another question, etc. The end resulted in an intriguing little toy laced with potential personal tidbits demanding innocent honesty of you. I don't remember much about that game or the specific time I played it, but I do often think about the point in the game where the "How many children will you have?" question would present itself like a rare Pokémon. I'd choose a number, the game host would open and close the paper toy the designated amount of times, and my fate was sealed.

I always chose four because I come from a family of six, so it seemed fitting to desire the outcome I myself got. Also, odd numbers freak me out, but that's something I'll leave for my therapist to dissect. The reason this question is particularly poignant (there were many others, of course) is because, even then, I couldn't picture myself with a wife, thus how could I imagine an adult life with kids in it? Even if by some biblical miracle I ever came out (surprise bitch! haHA), my destiny seemed to undoubtedly be different than any journey I'd ever come in contact with. It was scarce that I met anyone who was adopted and even more rare to find someone with two gay parents. The latter never happened, by the way. Well, it did, but it took two whole decades to do so. I met a boy who told me he had two moms while we were on a first date together. He was too cool and I attribute that fully to his lesbian upbringing.

The predetermined future presented to me on a single-item dinner menu at an extremely overrated restaurant was quickly deemed impossible in my young mind—impossible to plan, impossible to actualize, impossible to ever have for myself. And, that unsettledness made my prepubescent soul radiate six shades of queasy.

There were approximately 62,000,000 married heterosexual couples in all of the US in 2019. There were approximately 568,000 married homosexual couples in the US. That means 0.009 percent of all the couples you know are same-sex couples. I'm a numbers person, so researching those simple statistics blew my mind to smithereens. NO WONDER I FEEL SO ALONE AND CONFUSED . . . IT'S BECAUSE I KINDA AM. Not even kinda! If I'm lucky, I'm a 1/100? That's fucked! There aren't a lot of pathways to watch, study, and one day decide to wander down. Do you genuinely think I even know one hundred couples? Huh? Do you??? Gun to my head, I'm not even sure I can name the first and last names of one hundred individuals in my life. ALONE. All signs point to ALONE. I need to set out for a moment to gather myself before I lose the rest of this moldy muffin I call a mind. If there were a time to take up chain-smoking slim French Gauloises (don't look at me like that), now would be the optimal time.

Let's add some technicolor to the dooming statistics above. The past can eat shit in comparison to the promise the future holds for LGBTQIA+ people. It's nowhere but up from here. And, luckily, since many things have yet to be done by us (be elected president of the United States, be an astronaut who stands on the moon, win an Olympic gold medal in Solo Synchronized Swimming . . . well, just kidding, we all know ONLY gays have won that . . . I digress) the world is our oyster! If we flip the trope on its head, the act of never being here before means this experience really should be something exhilarating! There's unbound, infinite potential bubbling behind living the modern-day privileged LGBTQIA+ lifestyle. In a way, we all have been gifted a little of it purely by existing in these modern times. By growing up in the twenty-first century, with marriage equality, common workplace protection laws, and copious amounts of media representation, we're on our way toward the typical melancholic existence our straight peers currently have, and that our valiant elders have fought tirelessly for decades to obtain for us all. So, now that we're on the cusp of total equality, with it currently sliding across our calorically deprived taste buds . . . now what? Sis, we're basically here, what do we do now? You don't work for months to stop a few miles before a marathon's finish line. You cross it at all costs. No looking back. Defeat isn't even an option.

Don't get me wrong: The fight for equality across the board is never out of sight, and we have so much work to do, but things are better than ever. It's undeniable. And that progress breeds potential. And potential emits hope. So, I can't help but ponder what it's actually like to live a full gay life (coming to a theater near you!). Let's not entertain the mere concept of equality, but let's see it perform live in-person at its sold-out stadium tour.

As I wrapped up the final steps of my lengthy run, I approached the final hurtle in the form of a crosswalk hidden among blazing Los Angeles traffic. Every morning I approach this specific path, I wonder if the timing will be right. Will I land on this street in between red lights and engine silence or will it be during peak rush hour with horns blaring and rubber burning? Truth is, no matter the outcome, I know I can take the right-of-way. It's my virtue to pass over this hurdle, onto the parched concrete, and through these blurry, white lines. It may be dangerous. I may lock eyes with chaos. I could just as easily avoid this stress by pausing for a more relaxed moment. Or, on the contrary, I could assert myself, thrust forward, and speed onward toward my home nestled in the distance. A dangerous game is rarely won without taking a little risk.

Chapter Two

Tulip

Coming to curled up tightly on the edge of my couch; lit only by the remaining glow of the day's sun barely visible behind the February gloom. Shrunken so small into myself like a piece of arugula moments after resting on a scolding cast-iron pan, my eyes lift examining the room around me. I don't remember what got me here exactly, but I do know this feeling far better than I'd like to admit. Although it's not an uncommon feeling, and I very well know I've felt a similar shade of it way before, it does surprise me how unfamiliar a regular acquaintance can remain. This, however, feels worse than usual. Much worse, actually. Also, as if I'm paralyzed, immobilized in a stage of deep nothingness. I can't connect any of my thoughts; scatterbrained by my own mental state. My phone lies on the plush, white rug just below me (I haven't cleaned it in forever and being face-to-face with it would typically irritate me, but now I can't fathom caring). It must have fallen out of my hand as I drifted in and out of sleep. That tends to happen when I get this way. The day, or days if I'm particularly unlucky, meander by while I open and close my eyes. No hunger, no thirst, no desire to fix this messy state . . . a void.

I manage to pick up my phone and am immediately reminded I let someone know this was probably going to happen, by messages of:

"Oh no . . . Con, I'm sorry."

"Can I come over?"

"You're not responding . . ."

"I'm coming over."

Shit. I hate when I let other people know I've hit another depressive spiral. It's embarrassing. Even though I know it shouldn't be and my therapist reminds me otherwise every god damn appointment, it is. It makes me feel weak, helpless, a waste of everyone's worries. I have a habit of letting people know when it's gotten bad, but then swiftly refuse any help or rational words they provide, which always manages to make things even worse. It's like I've figured out how to reach out for help, but I still haven't quite figured out how to receive the help I asked for. This closed emotional circle fucking blows, and I hate bringing others into its dark, hopeless warp . . . ugh. I come out of my vacuum for a moment and am reminded my friend is on her way over. Seeing as both the gate and front door are locked, and I currently don't remember how to move my legs . . . it's safe to say I can't deal with this right now! Again, I'm going to say, this.fuck.ing. blows . . . and I'm . . . fuck.ing.use.less.

My iris shifts toward the clock. 3:30. Shit. How long have I been here?? What triggered me this time? I know it's hard to believe, but I honestly can't remember. Depression does that; fogs and even erases memories. Scientifically speaking. I'm sure it's some type of defense mechanism the body's resorted to, because for all intents and purposes, I'm not in any imminent danger on this couch, but the way I'm responding to my environment definitely personifies imminent peril. These thoughts may be metaphorical dangers, but technically speaking, they can't actually draw any blood, so I'm sure my body is fucking confused as to why this is happening. My own stupid brain hurting my own stupid body. WE'RE SUPPOSED TO BE A TEAM GUYS, DAMNIT . . . Oh yeah, she's on her way. Shit shit shit.

I'm not sure I can even communicate when she gets here. Is she going to try to talk to me? I hope she doesn't try to talk to me. I have nothing to say, and the things I could say have been said over and over before. New day, same story. I fade into sleep again and come to minutes later to the doorbell aggressively ringing. Uh-oh. She's here. Maybe my messages were more concerning than I realized. Hopefully I didn't scare her into thinking something bad was going to happen if she didn't come over. Fuck. I hope not. Fuck me. I hate myself. Why does this always happen?

Eventually, by nothing short of a biblical miracle and after far too many minutes, I crawl over to the door, unlock it, and make my way out to the gate to do the same. As it swings open, I'm greeted with a hug and no words. She's calm and warm—gentle with intention. All I can think is how disgusting I must look because god knows how long I've been in this mess of a mental prison. I want to apologize immediately, and I can feel the words at my lips, but again, I'm not sure I can speak, and if I do, I'll probably cry. I'm so weak. Releasing myself from her grip, lifting both corners of my lips quickly up

17

and down, I slowly lead her inside, plopping myself back down on the couch to continue my pathetic sulk. "I hate myself" is repeatedly written across my mind.

She doesn't say much, my friend. Although my eyes are on the floor, I can tell hers are combing the living room. What for, I'm not sure. She disappears into the house and soon returns with a blanket and a glass of water. Covering me fully, almost tucking me in like a mother does to her child at night, she places the water on the cream-colored coffee table beside me and we exist in silence. I wonder if she pities me. I look pitiful, that I'm sure of. In a weird way, I kinda want her to.

Her feet step onto the couch right behind the backs of my curled knees and she lowers herself down like a bird in its nest and tenderly rubs my side. Again, no real words have been exchanged, and I'm perfectly okay with it. She continues her attempt to comfort me in silence and I continue resting in my paralysis.

Shame fills my eyes and falls onto the cotton resting beside it. She rubs higher, now up on my forearm and back down onto my ribs. I can't tell if this is worse than when she wasn't here. Does pain hurt more when it's shared? Everyone says it doesn't, but it's impossible not to feel even smaller now. Like a forgotten tulip wilting in a vase, I coil tighter and tighter into myself, waiting to disappear in a quiet act of oblivion.

Time creeps by slower now with two bodies in the room. Her presence makes me aware of it more, so I suppose that is helpful. It should be, considering hours have slipped through my fingers like fresh caught salmon. She's still coddling me, but my cold reaction has forced her onto her phone, which is good. I feel bad enough she's here as is, let alone here and staring at a bare, white wall sending her into a solemn state of her own. Contagious depression. It saturates the air. After what seems like hours, but was probably much less, she asks if I need anything or if she can help in any way. I feel like a right dick because I still can't find words in my mouth. My eyes shift toward and dart away from her a few times in a noticeably awkward way. Just the thought of talking makes them wallow up a bit and I fear the pools will pour out if I unlatch my clenched jaw. I sort of shake my head conveying no, and although nearly unnoticeable, it was enough to be received in the implied way.

Truthfully, I don't know what else she could do. This is enough. It's MORE than enough, really. It's not like anything will cure this illness outright. It's not as if it's some sort of infection prescription antibiotics will rid me of in a few short days. I've come to realize over the past few years that when a storm like this hits, it must be ridden out. It's the only way to reach an end. The aftermath is when you deal with the destruction. If you can derail it before it reaches you, a technique I won't learn for a few years, then you're golden. But until then, it is what it is. So for the time being, with how bad these feelings are, I just have to wait until it passes. And in the meantime, I want to give my generous friend her life back. She's done an incredible kindness just by being here, and although it doesn't seem like it now, I am grateful. I am and she wouldn't care if I wasn't. She's a good one—present and willing to sink with me for a few moments—not trying to force any words out of me, no attempts to better me today. Just letting it be.

And although no resolutions were formed, I think this was more than I'd hoped to receive today. I'm so lost it's hard to know what I require to help. But this was part of it—someone to bear my weight and bring me back to reality even for just a second. A friend. She leaves silently and motions to message her later. I watch her walk from the shut door to the closing gate.

Its latches shut and my eyelids fall again.

four white walls

all this nonsense doing laps inside my head
moving time back on all the progress i've had

streamline up the sidewalk away from my own home
those four white walls echo the silence of a life lived alone

ghosts

i fall asleep with ghosts
i dream of them too
i wake up on my own
only soul in a home
once built for two

Chapter Three

An Attempt to Explain the
Unexplainable

These words are intended to befriend those who are burdened with heavy minds and to enlighten those who are fortunate enough to not bear that weight. Dark thoughts plague the minds of many—your friends, enemies, the driven, energetic, the sluggish, bright eyes, and toned skin. As unfortunate as it is, mental fragility discriminates against no one. We're all susceptible to its hollow elbow cradling our vulnerable throats. It's a silent companion, a quieter killer. As someone who has been inches away from falling victim to the misleading whispers and barren promises existing in my head, I would like to explain what it's like and share how I managed to liberate myself of that mental oppressor.

I would never in a million years classify my childhood or teenage years as bad, sad, or anything other than pleasant. I am a middle child who most certainly felt overlooked at times. I was a larger kid in a family of smaller people. I harbored a secret sexuality amongst counterparts with seemingly straightforward orientations. There was a certain "black sheep" element to my early years that ensured downward emotional moments, but that's all they were: moments. Fleeting and fading. This wasn't something that constantly corroded my cranium day in and day out. Like a star shooting across the night sky, the moments would arrive and depart in an instant. The more I marinate in those years, the more I remember how much love lay there. It's easy to highlight the worst, and let it overshadow the best. I try my best to not give in to that fraudulent temptation. Consistent cynicism only leads to dead ends.

Regardless of how I got there, I was there. The issue was obvious even though I didn't have the vocabulary to classify it. There were times I'd blink and it was dark again. The sink held a mountain of dishes. The bed idled unmade. My laptop rested open with no charge left in its battery. My skin had yet to meet the sun and my body had remained caged within four white walls. That's the depression I grew to know for years. The world moved around me while I felt still. There was movement in my life, but it mainly went unnoticed from my point of view. I had written several books, attended many weddings, or-dered expensive breakfasts on weekends, drank myself silly in the city, and stared awestruck at the starlight of the countryside as I took another hit of my friend's joint. Time passed. Memories were created. I wasn't dead, but I wasn't sure I was living either. My being was pres-ent, but somewhere else at the very same time.

For me, because mental illness glows in every color imaginable, depressive suicidal thoughts rotated around my head like a moon to a planet. Constantly. You know, I even knew I had everything good on paper, but nothing could shake me awake. I was like a rainbow trout with a sharp hook barbed deep into my lip; the harder I pulled and tugged at it, the deeper it sank in. Reeled closer and closer into a place I didn't want to be. Depression stalked me and suicide tried to consume me. But I never wanted it. Not genuinely. I may have fooled myself into thinking I did once or twice, but deep down, I knew that this ending had no beginning on the other side. That exit led to a pitfall. A stark plummet into dark nothingness. I couldn't do that to myself. I couldn't do that to the people that knew me. I couldn't. I wouldn't.

Suicidal thoughts ricochet in your head like a screaming baby on an airplane. They bounce from wall to wall for unknown lengths of time. There is no certain antidote. No guaranteed solution. You can tend to them all you want, but from my experience, it's a storm you have to ride out. The damage can be assessed only after the destruction occurs. I know that ain't pretty or what anyone wants to hear, but it was my truth for so many years. It's royally fucked up, really. You don't want to die, but it feels like the only way to stop the endless discomfort that comes with living. If you can't see a light at the end of a tunnel you're exhausted from sprinting down, it's only inevitable that you'll want to collapse. To rest. To give up. To quit.

Once I began to see the patterns of my mind, I realized it wasn't as clever as I once thought it to be. You fall into it suddenly. You fall out of it slowly. Like a foggy valley meeting the morning sun. This was always the case. So I just had to find a way to halt myself from the initial fall, to control and claim this life as my own. Bettering myself was a long, slow process with constant hiccups along the way. I wish there was a method I could share with you to take away your pain, but it's coded individually. Talking about it helps. Therapy is brilliant. Medication kept me from falling over and over again as well. Running did more for my stability than I can put into words. I added structure to my days and stability to my thoughts. I'm my most clear four miles into an eight-mile run. No noise. Few distractions. The world shifts into focus while I catch my stride, and keeps me in the light the remainder of the day. With practice I've learned to see thoughts as fiction. They aren't real and shouldn't be held to a high standard. If I notice I'm slipping into self-critical thinking, I clench my fist, and it reminds me to pivot somewhere more productive. It's the little things that build into massive change. Coming from someone who has seen the other side of this, the effort is worth it. Your pain is valid, and your future is worth meeting. Trust me.

seesaw

It's not that I want things to be easy, but do they

always have to be this hard?

Chapter Four

Saturated

Often, I get caught up in a thought spiral invoked by the overwhelming world seemingly flooding in around me. Where do I even begin?

Some people can afford to clone their dog, while others will never pay off their student loans. As I'm writing this piece, California is on fire, and Texas has completely frozen over. Sex workers are making millions with the help of digital media. Another city of homeless tents was erected down the street from my brother's house. People are eager to be informed on every nuance these modern times bring, and they'll ruthlessly berate anyone who makes a single mistake too. With increasing Wi-Fi speeds, you can keep your job and work remotely from anywhere around the world. There's a vegan option on nearly every restaurant menu I can find. Likes are a currency. Followers are too. Voters are continually suppressed. Minorities are as well. Sex still sells, but we still don't talk freely about it. Mental health is becoming less stigmatized, but it doesn't seem to make those who suffer feel any better. You can smoke marijuana outside a jail filled with people who sold it to your parents ten years ago. A black car can be summoned to your house with the click of a button. Your favorite takeaway meal will be there just as fast. People finally believe women, yet they still won't pay them an equal wage. Your next road trip can be powered purely by electricity, and your entire home can run on the sun alone. One country voted out a fascist egomaniac, while another was seized by a military coup. Modern medicine now allows HIV patients to live a full life for a $3 pill, but people in the US must pay $21,700 merely to call an ambulance. Facebook isn't cool, but TikTok now is. Kids become famous online when they dance for ten seconds and part their hair down the middle. Middle-aged women become infamous when they yell at strangers in the street. Oddly, it feels like everyone is gay, but that's not actually the case. You can wear whatever you want as long as you take seventeen photos of it. Pronouns should be below your email signature. People should not be judged by their past alone. We wear masks in public, but now they're physical too. Every morning there's a new cause to champion. Every night there's a new threat to lose sleep over.

Being a human in this day and age is a blessing and a curse. We have everything at our fingertips, but somehow manage to feel pretty empty inside. It's a lot. I validate how overwhelming it can be sometimes. Hell, most of the time. Let's be real. We've lost our autonomy to a global state of thinking, which was designed to be a positive thing, but it ends up leaving me wishing I were left alone more often. Leave me in the dark today. I don't want to know what's going on. It's not healthy to know everything all the time, but there's no escaping it any longer.

Sometimes I just want to toss my phone into a pool of dark water and run away into the woods. Free myself of it all. Liberate my mind from the connectivity that causes so much suffering. Escape the impending doom and hide from the growing list of global catastrophes. The catalogue of negatives gets longer and longer every time my finger swipes up.

Running away into a sea of evergreen and no cell service actually puts a smile on my face. I'm grinning from ear to ear like a deranged circus clown while I fall into that fantasy. I'd adopt a dog. Maybe even grow a garden overflowing with vibrant fruits and vegetables. There would finally be an excuse to whip out my mom's old sewing machine I swept away from Minnesota last year. The options are endless, and all I feel is peace toward leaving the madness behind. What a sweet dream in this beautiful nightmare.

But that's all it really is. A dream. A fantasy. At times, a fallacy even.

When I speak these concerns into existence, I'm uplifted by praise like "oh, I feel the same way." Maybe you do. Maybe we all do. Deep down somewhere in the swells of our guts, we know what isn't quite right and what is screaming of something so wrong. But we're too far lost in the rabbit hole to even imagine climbing our way back out. Community within tragedy doesn't provide an antidote, but it does make the sensation of drowning feel a little less lonely.

lost in the loop

shamed from sadness
lay to waste in these badlands
a story of self-sabotage
the paper inked in unnecessary guilt
yet i keep turning
every page stained all the same
i lose myself in the loop

friends with benefits

i became friends with the pain
although cold and harsh
it remained during the bad and the good
when all others had long left

Chapter Five

Small Puncture Wounds

All our words, actions, and events leave an unexpected lasting impression. This memory channel I'm about to walk down is a refusal to participate in a narrative I never chose to be a part of.

It's wild the distance my insides will go to blame undesired outside harms on my own self. Justifying the unjustifiable. This occurrence was really something that startled me at the time—like touching a fence without knowing it's electric—but its impact took time to take shape. There were many other small puncture wounds that I needed to tend to. The years 2014 to 2018 unknowingly contained the peaks of both my depression and my anxiety (as far as I know, that is . . . I'm no tarot card reader), so a stampede of wild horses raced across my mind and there were no pit stops in the madness. The pain was piling up, so how about another hefty helping, right? In our rawest of states, careless errors do tend to occur. Arrows fly the moment you rest your shield, and there's always a chance one will stick. Like a passing ship in the night, but with a Gaussian of hindsight, this tugboat was the *Titanic* after the iceberg, and I blindly ignored the destruction.

First, let's jump back in time a few years. My heart wounds were violently fresh after exiting an unhealthy relationship I, naively to be fair, thought could very well be my last. Not in a catastrophic way, but in a happily-ever-after type of way. This period has only become more clear as it ages, but again, in the heat of the moment, boy was I aimlessly lost and frighteningly broken during those crawling years. It's funny—prior to then, I'd never really been alone before. Like, truly left in my own solitude. Living, exploring, growing, and evolving simply by myself.

For the first eighteen years of my life, I was in a full household swaddled by family. The following two years, I was in a small university dorm room on a narrow hallway, closely quartered with fellow students. And finally, my first 1.5 years in California were spent living with multiple roommates in various spaces across the greater area of Los Angeles. So many boys. Way too much noise. Not a lot of time just for me. All of those moments led up to one summer day in August of 2015, aka the first year I signed the lease for my very own apartment, but coincidentally enough, I was deeply in love in my first committed relationship to another boy, so it never ever felt as such. Then, it ended and things suddenly changed. Up until this point, I always had some form of another human being physically by my side during all hours of most every morning, afternoon, and evening, yet now for the very first time . . . there was nothing but silence. A void occupied by myself, my thoughts, and all my heightened emotions.

I had forgotten what silence sounded like. It's deafening but so loud absurdly at the same time. All the little noises a house makes after the sun is gone roared as if a megaphone was held tightly to their lips. The quiet was ringing in my ears. So much so that I quickly developed a fear for it. A quick conclusion was made: I'd grown to loathe my own company, or less dramatically, forgotten how to enjoy it. I'd become so accustomed to another warm body illuminating the four-walled spaces around me my entire life, and this new recognition of seclusion was nothing short of frigid.

In an attempt to avoid myself, I surrounded myself with any other person who had a heartbeat and didn't mind a newfound, reserved introvert who somewhere along the line had misplaced his own social skills. Shockingly enough, people in Los Angeles LOVE to talk about themselves, so I easily accumulated a group around me at most any time of any day. Isn't avoiding your inviolable, fear-driven breakdown just wonderful? Whoever said new friends are hard to come by has never been a newly out twink living in West Hollywood. The truth is, I really hadn't ever been single and openly gay at the same time, so I had accumulated zero experience in how this world I'd thrust myself into actually worked—from the moment of realization to the moment of expression to the moment I made a video viewed by twelve million people that said, "HEY WORLD, LOOK AT ME! I'M GAY AS FUCK!" I had already been in a long-term relationship. So, fully reiterating here, I knew absolutely nothing about being a single gay man in a safe, affirming environment. I'm from the land of lakes, cheese, families spilling over with devoted Catholics, cornfields, and passive aggression, so if that doesn't paint the childhood upbringing equivalent of a Van Gogh in your brain, for what my level of life experiences was, then you kindly shut this book, douse it in lighter fluid, toss a match, and never think about me again . . .

This was supposed to have a tone leaning more toward seriousness, so let me exhale briefly, regather my thoughts, put back on my wig and large red nose, and walk back into the stage lights.

Very soon after I began settling into my new routine, I was introduced to a man in "the industry" with whom a colleague thought I would probably get along, so why not talk business together? The email title read "intro!" And I, with permission, was CC'd into a conversation. Eager to fill my calendar with work opportunities, I saw no harm in taking one on my own. It was standard and he seemed nice for words on a computer screen. A bit dry and a bit goofy in his mannerisms. There was an undeniable confidence in him too. While messaging back and forth several times, we decided to have a work meeting over dinner in walking distance of my house, so I agreed. Work discussion over food is fully expected in this industry, so to me, it was nothing more than an opportunity, or at the very least, a fancy meal probably comp'd by his company.

We met days later as planned, and things went well. I explained to him what I do, and we deciphered commonality amongst our fields, how they ultimately intersected, and the probability they'd intersect more in the less-than-distant future. He tossed ideas at me and I flung even more back at him. A classic game of capitalist tennis. The waitress came over and asked what drinks we wanted. I asked if we were drinking (alcohol, implied), and he informed me he was sober, but insisted, multiple times, that I drink anyways. After feeling the busy waitress's eyes piercing my skull, I ordered a cocktail and the dinner proceeded. We ate, talked, and left less than two hours later. To no surprise, we capped the night with the decision to stay in touch and figure out how to work more together. By all accounts, it was a success.

Over the course of the next month, we swapped messages here and there. I know we crossed paths at a work function, and perhaps a social event or two, but that timeline is fuzzy and I cannot remember all the specifics. I'd politely introduce him to whomever I was with, as you do. He'd ultimately do the same, and we'd part ways. Common manners and courtesies. So typical it feels stupid to write this out because I'm sure you're like "Uh, who cares . . . ?" Truth is, any exchange like this made me giddy. This man was a growing power in the industry and seeing a recognizable someone and introducing him to my friends made me feel some level of importance; a boost to my drained confidence. I had nearly identical feelings toward many other people I'd met since realizing loneliness tastes of rotting fruit months earlier, so to me this was normal. No work had actually come from it, but the idea of networking and feeling good about it was energizing. In entertainment, this cycle can become quite addicting because who you know is promise and power. Knowing the right people can get you places whether you'd like to believe it or not. It fucking blows to write that, but the truth ain't pretty most of the time.

This is why if you become an IMDb Detective after watching a good film, you MIGHT just find out that some of your favorite actors have suspiciously prominent relatives in the industry. What's that, a famous mother? Who's there, a decorated uncle? . . . coincidence? I'll let you decide.

Out of the fear you're beginning to yawn, I want to fast-forward. I'm not quite sure if it was a couple of weeks or months, but it wasn't too long. This connection was a blip in a full calendar year. Truly, we were dancing in the limbo of friends and acquaintances still. This is where I will place a written trigger warning for anyone reading who has past sexual-related traumas. This will be brief, but I need to say it.

One evening during that exploratory year as a newly liberated gay man, my friends and I decided to have a night out. Typically, we'd go to someone's apartment prior, listen to music, throw back a few doses of liquid poison, loudly gossip about our days, and inevitably make our way down to a half-mile stretch of gay bars on Santa Monica Blvd. The one thing I remember so vividly is that we were fresh into this location and the night itself. We made our way into one bar for enough time to have a single vodka soda, found it a bit lackluster, finished our drinks, and moved on to a livelier location down the street. Once in, surrounded by a gradient of men and soft darkness, we settled into the superior location swaying to the voices of female pop icons and yelling nonsense over the music. Not long after being here, I turned toward the open doorway to see a familiar face.

I'm sure you can piece together. Sober, industry, acquaintance man.

I smiled, yelled his name, and opened myself for a drunk hug. He stumbled over to me and strongly wrapped arms around me in a strange way I can't put words to, but it was immediately noticeable. I smelled the alcohol on his heavy breath and subtly made out the disorder in his eyes from the glow of the streetlights shining through the open doorway. As I released myself from his grip and twisted my body toward my friends to introduce him to those who had yet to meet him, things began to feel noticeably off. I could feel him still close to me. Uncomfortably close. My voice carried, and I was nodding. Everyone smiled as if they totally heard the name I'd just yelled over the blaring music. His arms gripped down from behind me. Why was he still behind me? He leaned down as if to tell me a secret, but clearly had no control over his intoxicated voice. "Come on, I know you like me. I know you'd like it. Come on." Confused as to what the actual fuck he was talking about, I laughed and said, "Uh, what do you mean?" Naive. He actually leaned in closely this time. So close. Too close. Lips-on-my-ear close. It felt as though he was thrusting against me. "I could make you feel so fucking good. I know you want it. I know you do." He shouted at my ear, loudly enough for half of my group to turn and stare at us with blank faces. I let out an awkward laugh, now visibly unsettled, like a mouse cornered by a large alley cat. "No, no really. That's okay. Let's go talk to my friends, or . . ." He kept his locked grip on me and pulled me in and out of his body.

My friends, still watching, were nowhere near tipsy enough to not know I was frozen in confusion and flooded with embarrassment. Quickly, I pushed away from the man, still laughing nervously with eyes wide on the ground. I moved to the other side of the circle. I wanted to evaporate. I wished I could melt into the fucking floor. Everyone was now uneasy and he was so clearly put off by what I had just done. He shouted nonsense and eventually staggered away. All the details after that are a blur. All I know is that within minutes, I left, and walked three miles home to quietly fall asleep. I felt weird, but I couldn't fully dissect those feelings to locate why. This was no time for me to dwell on anything, out of fear that I would fall into another depressive spiral. I'd been going in and out of them for months now, remember? Work was knocking at my door in the morning, and I couldn't afford not leaving my bed for a whole weekend. Not again. I didn't talk about that night in detail until just six months ago. It's been over three years. And, here I am.

I'm hesitant to fully place blame on anyone for that night, because in all seriousness, I'm unsure if that heavy burden is worth placing or bearing any longer. I'm not a malicious person. Hate will eat you alive. What went down on that night was clearly not okay, setting all interpretations and opinions aside. It all happened so quickly that it's nearly impossible now to place any blame on those watching for not coming to my aid or even a sober, industry, acquaintance man who clearly slipped to his knees because of many poor decisions that evening. It's complex. It's messy. But still utterly wrong. I don't want to debate any of that, but I do want to learn from how I feel now.

After confiding in my friend a half a year ago, I found out from her that this isn't an uncommon experience. In the US alone, one out of every three women have experienced some form of sexual violence. Ninety-one percent of all victims of rape and sexual assault are female. Although men are notorious for not reporting their own trials with abuse, assault, and trauma—something to keep in mind. Hell, twenty-five women accused a sitting president of the United States, Donald Trump, of various forms of sexual misconduct. This shit happens. Every day. In plain sight. It's not a secret. Oh, and it's only reported 5 percent of the time.

It's disheartening to hear how many people feel entitled to another human being, and it's frightening to know over half of those victimized know the perpetrator personally. Predatory behavior is vile. My heart breaks for a world where it exists so casually.

The only reason I write about this night is to hopefully open someone's mind to the importance of consent, and more importantly, to make those struggling with a secret, regardless of its weight, know that it can be lifted ever so slightly by confiding in someone you trust. I was already going through a rough time, and this man made it worse for me. He unknowingly pushed me lower than I knew I was capable of going. It made me question if every man was like this. Was this normal? Was I being ridiculous for not liking the attention? Was it so utterly strange for me to dwell on it more than a single evening? Can I trust people in my industry to only want to work together? Can I trust anyone without knowing their intentions? Will it happen again? How often does it happen? I'm drowning in singular questions. I'm overwhelmed by a storm in my head. Not that there is ever a good time for something bad to happen, but looking back, I think this was absolutely the worst time it could have happened. I was so vulnerable and alone. I'm not sure you can ever understand. Quickly, I closed the circle I was attempting to expand and I retreated from it.

One of the great ways to heal a bleeding heart is, oddly enough, by opening it up over and over again. But that wasn't going to happen for me for a long time. Seclusion met me with open arms. Isolation followed behind it. All those questions swimming in my brain made me know one thing for sure: I'm only safe if I never let anyone in ever again.

Days turned into months and months melted into years. I barricaded myself away from new people and kept a defensive stance with every interaction. There were times I would drop my fists in an attempt to start over, but they were short-lived. My mind would sabotage anyone who had the potential to be anything to me. I remember getting close to this guy . . . that is, until mid-hookup, the idea popped into my head:

What if this has been his plan all along?

Is this all he wants from me?

How can I be sure any of this is even real?

Maybe that's all he wanted. Maybe that's all I'm good for.

Those weren't thoughts I'd had prior to that night. That wasn't a fear I'd ever had before . . . that I was just some shell for someone to release their sexual energy around and lay me to waste afterward. I knew I was better than that. I knew I was worthy of more than that. Fuck anyone who treats anyone in such a vile way. I made a vague excuse to the guy in mid-hookup and left in a rush. I stopped seeing him soon after, with zero explanation as to why. That cycle of trying without success became the new normal and continued on with many more guys to come.

I feel bad about it still. How I was unable to explain why something seemingly good wasn't working over and over again. It made the cycle endless and made me feel hopeless.

Some memories we hold on to hold a deeper meaning than what we initially assign to them. After tumbling in an endless laundromat, and mulling that time over during countless late nights and long runs, I had an epiphany: I'm sick of allowing other people to maintain any control over my own future. No one and nothing, outside of my own self, should ever dictate, derail, or detain the time in front of me. I want better and I take it just as quickly. My emotions will not alter because of some set of actions flying at me like arrows in the daylight. My stamina will not fluctuate because of some series of events pouring into this moment in pure spontaneity. My efforts will not weaken because of some stream of words flowing from somebody's mouth like lava down the mountainside. I will not participate in it anymore. I'm done.

The truth is I could add any branch to this willow's narrative. I only feel like I'm strong because of my preexisting depression. He only acted that way because of alcohol. Worse things happen to people every single day, so why am I acting like an island plagued with drought? It doesn't matter now. It can't. I won't let it. It serves me nothing but a plate of long nights and lost potential. I could allow the creep who fondled me in my first gay bar to dictate how I treat strangers, or the old man who followed me to convention after convention after mailing me unsolicited gifts to keep me in hiding, or the stranger who showed up at my house demanding to come in because he thought we had a romantic connection to make me fear the world around me.

But I won't. Not anymore.

victim

I'm attached to the narrative like a fly to ripe

citrus. It's all I've ever known, or, at least, the only

self I've come to remember. The fruit is spoiling

beneath me. But I'm still latched on tight even

though I'm long overdue to drift away with the wind.

heartbreaker

i broke a heart just to know what it's like
played the role of the bad guy for once in my life
his eyes trace the corner of his doorstep
suddenly, i'm short of breath
like the grim reaper blowing a kiss of death
i haven't slept nor will i for days to come
tonight haunts me even though it was right

a sudden embrace

I saw the good side of life too early and there are

barely any secrets left to uncover, then I turn a

page and I'm embraced by my own ignorance.

Caught in a lie, but comforted by new potential.

polluted words

your speech is pollution
every word soaked in pain
we've gotten worse through evolution
intelligent, yes
but morality falls down in the rain

ouch

fucked up friends
left me feeling like
the fucked up friend

Chapter Six

Low-Hanging Fruit

Sitting front and center at a bar in Paris, I'm pivoting between reading a book, reminding myself of simple French phrases, and listening in on any ounce of English I can detect amongst the packed tables incubating my tiny North American body. Eavesdropping isn't considered polite by most standards, but sadly, I cannot help myself. You know what? No. I'll speak my truth. I'm a total slut for it. It's endlessly fascinating to drop into someone else's world for just a moment—a peek, the tiniest dip into another reality. Plus, it can be wildly entertaining to hear some out-of-context story. The way I see it, it's almost like fishing. You go about your morning or evening and wait until you sense a little nibble (in this case, on your ear), and you swiftly latch on before your catch fades back into the shadows. The two people seated a meter and a half away from me now begin a loud back-and-forth. A tennis match of shouting. I'm hooked, baby.

"WE ALL HAVE A SAD STORY WE'RE CONSTANTLY TELLING

THE WORLD," one friend says, beginning what seems like a speech to counsel her female peer. "He's depressed, she had an abusive father, they were assaulted, heck, I grew up in extreme poverty . . ." She throws her hands up in a cocktail of pure passion and visible frustration, pointing at fictional examples, but clearly drawing from real experience. "And, as soon as we're able to let go of that narrative"—she's poking her friend in the tit now—"THE SOONER WE CAN STOP LETTING IT DEFINE US."

The words leave her mouth with the same impact of a presidential inauguration speech. Resisting the urge to sit up and applaud her like a deranged psychopath, I divert my now locked eyes from the (private) conversation and back to the pages of *Cherry* by Nico Walker, and my mind begins to sprint as I take another swig of my cold draft beer.

Wow. What the fuck. I needed to hear that. Like, I really needed to hear that. That was fucking better than anything my therapist has told me in MONTHS. So honest. So raw. 99% on Rotten Tomatoes (it would have gotten 100 if she'd thrown back a shot and stormed out of the bar afterward). When we walk through the world, we don't tend to fixate on all its imperfections. If anything, we glaze over them. We avoid them. We pretend they don't exist. We naturally look for the good in most situations because socially we've been taught that that's what will gain us peer approval. Positive Paul is everyone's best friend, and Debbie Downer cries alone at her twenty-first birthday party. After taking a second glance at the metaphorical gorgeous park glistening a block in front of you, you see the cigarettes on the sidewalk, the dog shitting under the maple tree, and the woman screaming about the bugs in the air. Things are always better from a distance.

People are no different.

Just like the victim of my eavesdropping mentioned earlier, we all have a sad story to tell. Try to name one person in your life who truly has it all. Everything. The entire plate of croissants with not a crumb left behind. No suddenly deceased relatives, zero debt, a fully stocked refrigerator, hearty relationship with the parents, unshakable mental health, and a likable personality? Yeah fucking right! That's impossible! With every person comes baggage, and those bags come in a spectrum of colors. And we latch onto our issues and flaws like our entire identity depends upon it.

"I can't go out tonight because I'm feeling anxious."

"I don't need a date. My last breakup taught me one thing: I'm better off on my own."

"I grew up without any money, so please don't tell me how to use what I've earned now."

"I lost a friend in a car accident growing up, so I'll walk, thank you very much."

Those are vaguely poor examples, but I think you get it. I'm not sure when exactly these walls were built around us, but at the moment, they seem harmfully obvious. An unnecessary weight on our tired shoulders. We don't have to live by our faults. No one's keeping a tally. I find myself defining myself by an assumed definition more and more nowadays. I'm an introvert. I get anxious easily. Big parties are my worst enemy. Schedules are my best friend. My heart has been broken before, I don't need to keep putting myself out there. It's almost like I'm boxing myself in with a thunderstorm of asterisks added onto every aspect of every interaction. "I would never do that because . . ." "I would, but that's just not how I operate since . . ." Stop that! Cut it out! You are who you are in this very moment, and the rest leave to the history books.

My eyes rise slightly from the middle of the book to see a much calmer conversation wrapping up before me. The two girls are laughing and smiling and downing the remains of their chardonnay and giggling as they realize how drunk they are now. A paper bill is passed their way and they sign it just as quickly. I watch, openly now, as the two stumble arm in arm onto the street's cobblestones, smiling from their warm evening. They fade into oblivion, and my body swoons with tonight's potential.

glass ceiling

the glass ceiling is breaking
my darling
began like a hairline crack
from surroundings mistaking
we aren't under attack
be careful, my darling
the cake has been cut
and slices have been dealt
you see doors shut
but oh, my darling
this morning's worries melted away
they lay out at our feet
one for him, one for her
pieces for all to keep
we are broken apart
but become whole
when we stand together

Chapter Seven

Punchlines

How long do you want to continue to allow that to be a part of your narrative? How much longer are you willing to attach something negative or harmful to your story's opening credits? I have depression and I have anxiety, but how long am I willing to let them, and other things like them, rule my life? At some point, you have to ask yourself: Are you giving your demons too much power? Are the things you hate about yourself becoming the headlines to your conversations, the punchlines to all your jokes, the suffocating bullet points to your every waking moment? When will you stop giving them a voice?

I'm starting to recognize this as a bad habit or as misguided intentions. At first, calling out something I was once insecure about was a form of social therapy. HA! I SAID IT FIRST! BEAT YOU TO THE PUNCHLINE! IT'S NOT AWKWARD NOW THAT I'VE TAKEN CONTROL OF THE NARRATIVE! There's truth to those intentions.

Calling out a problem I was internally facing did help me become more comfortable with it for a while, but I've noticed a tipping point in that practice. Words like *depression* and *anxiety* soon moved from one punchline to every punchline. These "jokes" shared in solidarity soon became something I would share with near strangers. "Haha! Well, could be worse . . . you could be plagued by daily depression!" I once loudly shouted amongst a group of people I'd just met at a friends-giving. It didn't land well. We had literally just met. The practice that built my confidence back up began to tear it back down again.

Not to sound utterly foolish here, of course. I'll wipe the meta-phorical egg off my face while I say: Obviously, ignoring your diag-nosed OCD or bipolar disorder isn't going to magically get rid of it. But screaming about your chronic stress at brunch in East Portland isn't going to make it go away for good, either. There are children here, Samantha . . . Jesus. The way we approach modern mental health struggles and contemporary clinical compulsions carries a fresh bag of nuance. It's okay to joke about an experience if you have experi-enced it yourself, right? If everyone who's a part of the conversation has something traumatic in common, then it's a feeding frenzy—all political correctness is off the table and we'll go buck wild with the only intention to shock, right? Don't joke about wanting to kill your-self in front of your Republican relatives and an amputated Fraser fir toward the end of December, right? It's not rocket science, right? There's a special way to go about these conversations, and really, an entire book could be written on the topic. Heck, people weren't even mentioning their issues in the eighties, let alone screaming about them over overpriced eggs benedict. Growth redefines itself without permission.

Chapter Eight

Everything or Absolutely Nothing at All

You know that decade squeezed in between the small window of adolescence and the immediate crisis that follows? Yes, that one. Yeah, it's undeniably fucked up. Your twenties are something else, man. They make you feel hopeful, hopeless, excited, depressed, insane, and grounded all at the same time. You run around the world thinking you're an invincible, nasty little shit one minute, and suddenly you wake up the following Tuesday in January to your fucking head being cut off and thrown across the room. No . . . literally. Legit, that happened. I read an article the other day about a girl who cut her cheating boyfriend's dick off and threw it into the hallway. Sick but . . . justified? I'm no judge, but I sure as hell am judge-y.

I'm seven years into this slice of life cake, and I'm curious to know if everything has always, or God I hope not, will always be this eclectic? Have things always been this difficult, or can I attribute my constant confusion to the smartphone in my pocket, unregulated chemicals I'm ingesting daily, threat of global nuclear holocaust, Earth's impending climate collapse, or the awkward length my hair is currently at? Do I shave my head or does nothing really matter because we're going to die—JUST THINKING OUT LOUD HERE. It's difficult to imagine a time where these feelings aren't all over the place. It's almost as if Pandora's box has been opened and there's no way to unsee what it contains. I've shaken hands with the Devil, and no matter what I do, Hell is on the horizon. That sweet, savory umami flavor of nihilistic doom. Mmm. Delicious.

I can't decide if it's comforting to know that most other people I meet in this demographic have also previously felt, or are currently feeling, a similar type of way—depending upon which notch they currently fall on its belt. That's also the fucked up part of this age range, because so many important milestones exist and everyone can be on a different page than their similarly aged counterparts. Like, for a while there, it was difficult to relate to my friends back home because they were all still in school. Either studying to obtain their undergraduate degree, or taking a step further to claim their coveted master's degree. It's actually quite difficult to find commonalities between us when I'm a person who dropped out of school, moved to a Top 5 Major American City, and got financially lucky by yelling at a cheap, black tripod for a few minutes a week. Meanwhile they're studying until their eyes bleed nightly in the freezing Midwest, and their student loan debt might burden them until their kids are in the same position (FUCK THE U.S. EDUCATION SYSTEM, RIGHT?). I'm not looking for pity for either of us, because neither is the better choice. Yes, sure, mine sounds lovely now, but who's going to be laughing twenty years from now, when I'm poor, high off my roommate's burnt dollar store marijuana before I've had breakfast, and still babbling to a camera in my bedroom about "10 Tips for Living Out Your Wildest Dream"? HUH? And they're the married, tenured college professor with a stable mortgage, new puppy, and nice *Bon Appétit*–inspired food for dinner.

Jokes aside, that's simply one, small facet of this time period. I've met people who are still wearing the same athletic T-shirt I saw them in when we were teenagers. A certain musician seemingly out of nowhere became the biggest star in the world months after we ate cold beans on a couch in Venice. Out of the blue, another someone was diagnosed with schizophrenia after setting his living room on fire, and this was after we drank mid-shelf red wine while watching some bogus awards show. Everything can happen—or also, absolutely nothing at all. There lies the excitement. There lies the terror. There lies a sample of the many peaks and the many valleys you might go through. Scared yet? I am.

None of this is said with judgment or to knock any one person's choices. Who am I to think one life is better than another? That's ridiculous, and humans shouldn't be compared. For all we know, the person who has kept his/her life exactly the same for the last decade is much happier than the person whose life exploded into an international commodity. I just find it very interesting that both are possible in such a palatable amount of time. Granted, one might take chance, timing, luck, and many other things, BUT it still happened, which of course, sends my mind into a tizzy. Is potential limited? At what point do you give up and try a new direction? Should we strive to find comfort, and what level is bad? So many unanswerable questions . . .

For me, one of my greatest and more fearful questions is: Will it ever be enough? Or, alternatively, will I ever be satisfied enough with where I'm at or what I've got or who I'm with? Anyone out there have chills reading that? Is it twisted if I think, *I hope so*, while sitting here writing this? I do. But only because I want to feel less singular in this human experience.

That makes it all sound depressing, and I swear on my loved ones' lives (without permission, consent, rights, warrants, or a completed education), it isn't. To be perfectly blunt: This shit doesn't have to be bleak, and it surely doesn't have to feel twisted a majority of the time. I think what's peaking on the daily difficulty list is that we obsess over the bad portions of this experience; they're so heightened, blunt, so poignant and fresh. Everything seems to fall on the highest or lowest ends of the scale, and I think that's because there's little to compare it all to.

Have you ever taken a long road trip to a new destination? We're talking snacks a-plenty and three pee stops, MINIMUM. The drive there always seems longer than the drive back because there's less to experience the second time around. Now imagine you go on that same journey frequently, say once a month. After a year of voyaging, every nook, cranny, twist, and turn soon will have become familiar; you easily compare the travel times and now know how to better pass the hours (and where the ideal pee stops are . . . but that's beside the point). Hardship and triumph are no different. Neither tastes quite as sweet or as sour the more it passes your lips. That's a large lesson your twenties bring, and that's why it's so important to fly and fall as much as possible during this time.

Again, I must reiterate here: I have zero clue what the fuck I'm doing most of the time. Zero. Zilch. None. Nein. Nada. The case has run dry after no clues were found. The closer I get to my thirties, the more I begin to wonder if any of this gets any easier. When are things going to mellow out a bit? Will a destination ever become clear or am I waiting for something that never occurs? I'm sick of everything always feeling like life or death, high or low, valuable or worthless. There's an odd craving I'm beginning to taste for things to be more straightforward, color-coded, and clearly labeled (preferably in a vintage aluminum filing cabinet like the ones my parents had in our basement until 2012). Again, when I talk to other twenty-somethings, this feeling is fully mutual, so I suppose it's nice to know we're lost in the fog together. My friend in Minnesota may have found her life partner, but she's not happy with her debt or location. My friend in the United Kingdom may have hit it big financially, but he has yet to direct the film that will set off his career in the direction we all know he'll only be happy if it goes.

We're all here, we're all tired, and we're all just trying to get over one hurdle to make our way to the next one. It ain't pretty. It's not what anyone wants to hear. But, like most things, it is what it is. And something about that ambiguity brings peace to my chaos.

4 am

blasted in the street
searching for a stranger
left a club down the back alley
four hours stolen by a rager
white lines and sweet limes
sour faces and wet spines

we're lost in a techno song
no one will soon remember

bad mornings follow good nights
watch me stumble through the haze
drink any liquid in my hand
a warm smile still has bills to pay

we fade away with the stars

6 am

silence envelops the room with a honeyed aroma
warmth, a familiar face in a crowded room
streetlights hum before daybreak
calm, a bath of resting water
hope awakens an inception within me

quantitative suffering

Your pain is not deemed insignificant because

other people have a greater significance of pain.

grooves

two bodies
lie within each other's grooves
sinking into one another
like a wick into warm wax
they melt at dawn

dance around the gardens

the roots of the truth bury deep inside
quarter-eyed boy with nowhere left to hide

finally facing himself for the very first time
releasing that dagger plunged into his side

it's terror, it's freedom
a rebel leading a revolution

and nothing can prepare him for the instability that follows hardship
but one must persevere through the darkness and dance around the gardens

this moment right now is all he's ever wanted

Chapter Nine

Super Nostalgia

Sunday morning cartoons echo from the basement and football chimes from the cream-carpeted living room above. Parents cheer for the Green Bay Packers' touchdown while children lost in an animated realm roar as Goku punches Frieza. Both battles hold a multitude of heavy stakes. Froot Loops, Eggo waffles, Minute Maid orange juice, and white skim milk sit scattered across every surface the kitchen has to offer. Energy pours out of us like a loose telephone wire jumping in the street. And yes, you'll have to call a professional to contain either of the two. The windows radiate like fire from the maple leaves showering our backyard. Frosted exhales float up into the air to meet the clouds drifting by above. Smells of damp earth and ripe fruit saturate around us. With mitten-covered hands and Nike sweaters on our backs, we rush through the neighborhood howling and giggling and running amok. Everything is simple and easy in autumn of 1998.

I loved my childhood dearly, and I look back on it fondly. If anything, the appreciation grows for it the older I get. And, it grows even further the more I hear how isolated past pleasantries can be for some people, sadly. Nevertheless, mine live rent-free in my heart and in the back of my mind. To this day, the past halts me dead in my tracks. A smell, sound, sight—you name it. Something as simple as a caramel apple can flash me back twenty years into the past. Like I'm at a drive-in movie, and my adolescence is being mistily projected on a screen three rows ahead of me. It's overwhelming sometimes, you know? Thinking about how you couldn't go back to it no matter how hard you tried. A desire to do the impossible, even though you know it to be so. You can never quite recreate something that's already been done before. The exact setting, down to the old, tan couches your mom hated. The inexperience you had containing your small world and keeping your horizons hidden. And the feelings once omitted from your skin that made it all so visceral and vibrant. A sun within your very own personal universe. I remember any argument with my older brother felt like my entire life was crumbling in around me. The cause of the altercation didn't matter, and neither did the justification. When we fought, everything else froze. Brazen. Animated. Uncertain. Loud rage and pain to match. Things could break down in an instant and be built back up just as quickly. Every day was singular; rarely did emotions carry over from the previous. When you're young, your reality exists in a vacuum.

Typically, when I think of nostalgia, outside of actually feeling it, I associate it with beauty. I've always regarded it as pleasant, but lately, a strange sense of agony is attached to it. The pain of knowing things will never be as they once were. It's mourning, really. My past self is dead. He's gone, and won't ever return. I don't even really like the guy that much compared to the person I am now, but I can't help but cry over his surroundings. The still hometown where we kept our doors unlocked at night. The friend circle that made me feel like I needed no one else in the entire world. The routine of school, sports, homework, weekends, competitions, and holidays, which fell on repeat for eighteen years straight. Less worries about what processed food was going to rot me from the inside out. More cares about if we were going to get tickets to the midnight Harry Potter premiere, and equally as important, if we could get the bar seats positioned just above the empty aisle. I thought about what I looked like, I cared about my appearance just as much as the next nineties kid. But I didn't seem to catch my reflection in a glass screen every five minutes like I do now. I'd wear the same black North Face fleece jacket morning, noon, and night because nothing could ever be better or cooler. We'd meet to watch a movie every weekend at the friend-who-had-the-largest-television's house, as if it were the very first time we'd seen it. Comedy films have never hit the same since. That's a damn fact. If there were other things to do in a teenager's life, we didn't think to think of them. As far as we were concerned, we had everything. What more could we possibly want? Reality was contained; I walked through it with the glow of a candle only illuminating the path in front of me.

Rose-colored glasses are clearly at play here. Things weren't perfect, and clearly could always be better. When you're rich, poor, dumb, smart, winning, or losing, the grass will without a doubt be greener on your neighbor's lawn. With super nostalgia racing through my veins, I let all of my past impurities sink into the ground below me. I see my happiness through the lens of a Super 8 camera. It existed there. I can feel it. Fuck man, I can feel it. I yearn to hold hands with yesterday's memory.

There's love here in the present though. Don't get me wrong. I carry who I've become with pride. We weathered many storms to get to a place of peace, and discounting that journey would be an unrighteous act against self-improvement. Moving forward is a courageous leap of faith. I've seen one too many people get stuck marinating in the past, and they lie there still. Suspended. Soaking. With envy and contempt, I reject that way of life for me as well.

But maybe I should just give in and allow myself to fall. To grieve what once was, so I can fully uplift what actually is. I'm much older now. It's frightening to walk farther and farther away from what you know, toward an unknown future. That's it right there. I fall into the past like a pillow-top mattress. I ease into it like walking into cool water. Step after step. Slowly but surely. Eventually, you must give in, and allow yourself to go under.

temporary

This can't be it. This can't be everything.

Am I the only one let down by my own

inevitability?

borrow him

summer in saint denis
hidden behind simple delights
diving into deep disturbia
i want to borrow him until tomorrow
stolen but please stay with me
just for tonight
all i ask is for the night

marlboro

french with a boy in florence
walked him through the louvre
general store liquor and table wine
if i had a dime for all the times
i fell in love with those brown eyes

marble and a pack of marlboro
we rolled into the noon hours
hate to smoke but i light it just for fun
we're invincible and we're young
a couple kids kissing under the sun

exhausted after an exhale
we've fallen into this too soon
wrapped around his finger like a wedding ring
plucking at my heartstrings
but we're just another summer fling

i feel guilty knowing this will never last

i am my own loneliness

i felt alone before him
i felt alone with him
i felt alone without him
maybe it's me

Chapter Ten

Longing

I'm constantly worried I live too safely, cradled in bubble-wrapped arms that shield me from any pain, threat, fear, or annihilation.

When you're young, there's a certain freedom that comes with the implied ignorance. Beauty attaches to inexperience. That's why you're fearless. It's why you feel indestructible, even. A metal body bursting through time and ricocheting off the atmosphere. Really— and it pains me to say—you have no idea of your own fragility. It hasn't met you. You have yet to see a brittle body staring back at you in the bathroom mirror. And until that moment occurs, it's fiction.

I long to regain that feeling in my twenties, but can see it slipping through my fingers like sand. I want to jump from high places. I want to get mindlessly drunk on a Tuesday. I want to run full speed across iced-over lakes. I want to drop acid at a cabin in the middle of Yosemite. I want to ask someone at a coffee shop out. I want to move across the world. I want to meet up with a stranger and have careless sex. I want to go back to school and learn a new profession. I want to drive my car fast along the stretch of the 101. I want to quit and start all over. I want to live dangerously like today is my last. I want to. I do. But, it's so fucking hard when you know the consequences of your actions. As much as we'd like to believe, we lose our individuality as we grow and as we connect closer with the more permanent circle of loved ones around us. The actions of myself are repercussions for all who know me. My risks affect their peace.

Oh, how sometimes I wish I didn't know any better.

Chapter Eleven

The Anatomy of a Flower

I knew I was gay from a young age (like many people). It was a part of me from the very beginning. Sugar is sweet. The sky is blue. Soup is eaten with a spoon. Even at eleven years old, it was as clear as day. This facet of my character made total sense and fit with me like that first puzzle piece. I've laid out that story time and time again, so I won't repeat it ad nauseam. But with all honesty, I must remind you: It's the only reason you're reading the words on this page today. My acceptance of self pushed me into a new lane of life. Have you ever been so bad at bowling, the ball flew into another lane? Well, that ball was me. I'm a newly directed bowling ball at the fate of gravity and poor upper body strength. I landed into an alternate timeline that only bloomed out of vulnerability. It's disservice to not acknowledge my beginnings.

Yet, what I've learned seven years later—post coming out to the public—goes much deeper than those three terrifying words: *I am gay.* Oh, honey. Sweetie. Darling. Boo-boo. If I'd only known that leap would be a catalyst toward much deeper discoveries. It was only a drop in the bucket. A flake of glitter on the carpet. A teaspoon of vanilla in the birthday cake!

Okay, I may be getting caught up in the rhythmic drama of typing.

But shit did get real, real quick.

What people rarely discuss is the vital depths of community culture, and how acceptance goes far beyond one's self. To be different, you accept difference. When joining the LGBTQIA+ community, visually you'll understand: There's a lot to direct there! The L. The G. The B. The T. The Q. The I. The A. And, don't you dare forget, the motherfucking +! We're a family of societal misfits. A collection of traditional rejects. So, naturally, there are many colorful stories to hear and journeys to learn about. Being different isn't what history paints it to be. It doesn't make you wrong. It doesn't mean you're less than others. We're finally evolving to the place where the vast population understands that, but the work is nowhere near complete.

After I came out, I truly thought, *Okay, I'm gay now. That's it. We're done here. Time to date a man, and continue on with everything else staying the same.* Shh, shh, poor, naive, fragile twink. You're back to square one now. There's much to learn.

Queer culture is like another language. No, really, we have a different language. Top, bottom, twink, bear, discreet, fruity, demi, dom, you name it! Dot the eyes and cross the tees. Signed, sealed, delivered—I'm yours!

Now, I'm not Bill Nye the Sexual Guide Guy. This chapter isn't going to define everything for you. You have Google; look it up! But, what I'm trying to say is, I walked out of the closet and into a classroom. I had a lot of terms, stories, and people to learn about because their journey was now a part of mine (as mine was theirs). That's what community is all about. We walk into tomorrow, together. Soon, I began to discover more about the individual I was ultimately meant to be.

I'm not much of a partier or a hyper-sexual person. It's difficult for me to imagine being anything but a vanilla monogamist long-term. I'm mainly attracted to men, but I have found myself infatuated with many gender-nonconforming people over the years. It feels weird to point that out, because people are just people, and ironically, I don't particularly like to categorize them. When I'm in love, I have tunnel vision. The person I'm with is the sun, and I can't look away even though my eyes are burning. There's no way I could cheat on someone. I couldn't do it if I tried. I'm like a puppy obsessed with the person who brought me back home, and my only goal is to hug and cuddle. Hookup culture terrifies me and intrigues me. I've tried it and liked it. I've tried it and felt strangely dirty afterward as well. Usually, I've been celibate for months when those feelings hit for some unknown reason. Kissing strangers is undeniably electric, but kissing someone you love is unexplainable. There have been times where I've been called a faggot, simply for walking down the street. And I learned words could hurt for years. There have been times when someone from a passing car has yelled at me, simply for holding my boyfriend's hand outside a restaurant. Sometimes I think I'm demi-sexual. Other times, I think Catholicism and traditionalism have rotted my brain into thinking sex is evil, and those who have it are dirty. Part of me wants to rebel against that and consensually sleep with everyone in my whole fucking neighborhood. For over a decade, I prayed to a God I didn't believe in to make me like the rest of my friends. Fast-forward to the present day, and half of those people have come out as queer themselves. Guess wishes do come true, or maybe the divine has a sense of humor.

Identity is complex. There's no way around it. The deeper you allow yourself to dive into it, the farther down the rabbit hole you'll go.

I often wonder if I've overcomplicated something that could be made much easier. Looking at the lives of my siblings or the farthest members of my friendship circle, my entire being cycles into a thought wave of: Could I ever have what they do? Not simple, but by appearance, definitely much less complicated. There's much less nuance to a heteronormative existence. That's not meant to belittle heteronormative people by any means. Truth is, though, a road map exists for these people.

For me, and people like me, there is much less to go off of and many more struggles to be had just for merely existing. Do they (my straight counterparts) too get caught up in these identity crisis daydreams while out for a walk at sunset? Is it normal to question literally everything all the time? Am I alone here? Is this experience granular? I can't answer that. Hell, clearly I continue to question it all even after figuring most of it out. I'm not sure anyone can with full honesty figure it out. They'd be lying if they thought they could. As long as society creates an "other" category, these ostracized complexities won't be given endless amounts of fresh air to breathe in. An "other" only exists because someone declared another the "norm." That's all really. One day someone said, "A man marries a woman." Another someone said, "We only love one person, marry them, procreate two times, beg for forgiveness, then die." And the world has followed blindly ever since. It is as it always has been. Don't question it.

But that's all fiction. We take in fallacies as children and only undress them in adulthood if we're lucky. Someone in the past could have just as easily decided the reverse to be true, and this world could have been flipped so that straight was abnormal and gay was normal. What if we lived in a world where difference was embraced and not rejected?

Joining the LGBTQIA+ community widened my horizons to infinite possibilities the span of the galaxy and beyond even that. If I can exist as I am, who's to say everyone else can't as well? As long as who they are and what they identify with isn't harming or discriminating against others, of course. My twenty-eight-year-old motto is to embrace curiosity, and I no longer react to surprising encounters with fear, negativity, aggressive confusion, or any shape of hatred. I relate to them much more ever since living a version of them myself. It's basic human empathy, really. There shouldn't be anything special about caring for the fragility that is human life.

Back in 2014, I knew I was going to come out, but I had no idea I'd continue walking forward into a new version of myself. That end forged new beginnings again and again and again.

spring

a hatched mind buds before it blooms
after healing cleanses all its hurting
still spying a few blue wounds
that burn a bright bonfire
spring roses thaw below robin eggs
the world welcomes the new you

blueprints

i want to do all the wrong things
quit fighting with the right things
sometimes the good things
leave me feeling nothing
i don't need to be everything
but only just a big something
who decides all the wrong things
can never be the right things
it's time to change something
to relieve me of this nothing
before everything falls apart

daybreak

nightfall
clawing at the earth
dirt accumulates behind my nails
sprinting up an incline
into puddles and over rivers
gasping for some relief
lungs resemble empty balloons
a tree collapsed
longing to be its friend
i'm dizzy and falling into space
forks form and i choose a path
split-second decisions dictate a lineage
following the curve of a never-ending path
how much longer can i bear it
every nerve, tested
giving up is never an option
daybreak

mental strides

therapy comes in the form of a stride
ink on paper, an exhale of my mind
i find myself the more i get lost in these pages
a wild horse let loose in the races
watch me sprint down main street in search of today

fighting back

It quickly became the most important part of my

life. To find clarity. To obtain growth. To center

myself in peace. I no longer wanted to live in fear

of existing impartial as I was, so I had no choice

but to change. To die today would be a gift. But in

outright refusal, I began a quiet revolution. And

threw my first punch back at the world.

Chapter Twelve

Claude Monet

"**D**inner's served at seven. Don't be late!" our guide said as we retired for an hour of silence to clean up after a long, yet lovely day on an African safari. Our seven-day explorative and educational trip just outside Nairobi, Kenya, was coming to an end, with tonight being our last. The previous week had been flooded with volunteering: building a library in a neighboring village, touring the recently constructed health clinic up the road, visiting the new all-girls educational facility, studying up on the organic gardens currently being harvested in a nearby patch of fertile land, hearing the tales and the stories of local Masai warriors, and so, so much more. What a whirlwind of an experience it'd been. I was exhausted in all the right ways, and not just from running across the open savanna with my machete-wielding guardian, Wilson.

"Wilson, are there lions out here?" I had asked, jokingly rushing in the open.

"Of course, sir!" he replied with a smile.

"Oh," fell out as quickly as my eyes widened into quarters.

Wilson gleefully sprinted ahead in his sandals, leaving me in the dust.

Walking out of my small, softly lit tent equipped with an outdoor shower, sink, toilet, and bed, I emerged clean from the day and ready to indulge in the many foods the locals shared with us upon our return each evening. I felt utterly spoiled being here, and there wasn't a lack of gratitude expressed at every bend and corner. The evening air was brisk, laced with a gradient of natural noise from the various creatures and critters lurking in the foliage around me. The sky was colorful and my heart officially had fallen to a rest rate. Euphoric. Bumping into several of my fellow travelers along the way down the dim, cobblestone pathway, we walked and talked about our day, but mainly about the meal soon to be had.

Every night prior to this, the dining area had been swimming with relaxed bodies and liberated words. We were taking in so much new information on these sunup-to-sundown days that once we made our way here night after night, we were finally allowed to digest all that had occurred for both us individually and as a collective. All our takeaways, thoughts, reactions, and feelings could finally breathe life into conversation amongst a group of people I had only met once my feet touched down in this place for the very first time one week ago. Admittedly, I was accompanied by two of my closest friends, but still, you get the picture.

It was an odd thing to feel so close to seeming strangers so suddenly. Never in my life had it happened as quickly as it did here. We bonded like flour with water and grew close like a vine up a brick wall. Tonight, our bond finally became clear and it was something special. The group of twelve aligned together through experience, brutal vulnerability, open hearts, and a shared desire to do something with our newfound knowledge. We had witnessed the power of human connection and communal change together, and it felt almost impossible not to feel intertwined spiritually—religiously even (a vulnerable statement from a recovering Catholic).

We sat around a long wooden dining table under a high straw roof, but still remained open to the wilderness around us. The night sky creeping in was softly lighting up with stars. The color from the shifting hours accentuated their glow like perplexing strokes from a Claude Monet painting. Picture in your mind a whimsical, storybook treehouse. Like a Wes Anderson film had a baby with a Disney movie. We were sitting in it, baby. Bats were flying in and out of our vulnerable shelter, transfixed by the lighting fixtures above and the many moths fluttering around them. A meal was being had above ours.

"Dinner is served," one of the culinary assistants said in a whisper behind a smile.

We left the table to fill every inch of our white plates. Vegetables, rice, sauces, salad, meat (that I couldn't have), oh me oh my. Heaven has a name and it is buffet. We played a form of musical chairs every day in order to fully become familiar with each member of our group, and tonight's "game" was our last, which made us all feel a certain sadness. Seated with one of the girls on my right and guys on my left—although by this point we all knew one another very well—we ate, chatted, and discovered new facts about these not-so-strange strangers one last time.

I'm sure by now you're curious as to what the point of this vividly descriptive chapter is. Don't worry. Be patient. We're nearly there.

Laughs were had and our last meal was devoured. We sat around, sipping our drinks in pure contentment. Without even exchanging words about it, I think the thought slowly began to dawn on us all: The adventure is over, and truth be told, things for us may be as well. The reality set in that none of us knew one another in the "real" world for a reason, mainly geographical. One lived in Toronto, one in London, another in New York City, Los Angeles, and so on. As much as we'd grown close, it was difficult to imagine this bliss beyond the uniqueness of this location. It was impossible to think more than ten strangers could continue this. We could try. But would we? Most of us quickly knew this was an oasis; something unprecedented had occurred before our very eyes that would not and could not live beyond the present. Now we must each silently decide: Do we accept it or do we fight for it?

The drinks continued to pour and the night fell further around us, moving this day into the next. Knowing the current state of us, a strange thing began to occur. The group that had shocked me with their candor and honesty became even more so. Someone suggested aloud that we share something with the group that no one else knew about each of us. Genuinely a frightening concept. Fear found its way down my spine and into the hairs growing out of my forearms. I knew we all would take this task seriously. I mean, it wasn't some cheap party game you play with a few drunken pals and no one actually follows through. If we all agreed, it would happen with full transparency. So, as someone who harbors many secrets, I quietly sighed to myself: . . . *shit*. And, the game began.

Just as I'd assumed, this was no "game" at all. This was real. This was brutal. Like a breakpoint in a therapy session. People began to share stories of scars, private pain, and quiet torment aloud with the masses.

"I think my best years are behind me, and I'm slowly losing all the potential I once had. Everyone around me seems to be excited about their future, but as hard as I try, I can't picture making it to mine," a young, quiet girl in the group softly spoke. Her voice shook as every word left her mouth.

"My parents will never accept me for who I am, and it haunts most hours of most days. They don't even know me. The real me," another girl shared in visible sorrow from the opposite end of the table.

"All of my friends seem to have it together—jobs, partners, futures—and I feel like they're slowly leaving me behind. I don't know what I want. With anything." One of our adult male guides suddenly joined into the session. Secrets now fell on the table like orange leaves under a maple tree in October.

"I'm terrified I'm wasting years of my life thinking about someone who no longer thinks about me," I finally said, with my eyes on the floorboards. Tears dripped through the cracks, and my neighbors rubbed circles on the center of my back.

In a place full of what seemed like joyous souls with everything to live for, there was a collective aroma of uncertainty pooling around us. These people, all publicly successful, were haunted by demons. No matter how small we could belittle them into being, to their owner they undoubtedly towered above them with venom and ferocity. They suddenly wore their pain. I saw it in their eyes and now-altered body language. Some unable to face the group. Others lost in bad memories with eyes totally glossed over. Most had participated and were feeling the effects. Silence enveloped this space, and I began to feel like I was hovering behind myself watching this unfold so suddenly. Our last night together, exhausted and pleasant, now turned a bit sour.

There was beauty in this chaos, no doubt. We lifted the curtain and the magic show suddenly felt less than, but in hindsight, it was all nowhere near that simple. Emotions are complex and sharing them can be a trauma in itself. But the truth holsters power, and it's often not what the world wants it to be. Whether it be the bravery to walk truth into the light or the strength to claim it as your own, it takes grit to live in sincerity. Many try, some fail, but most turn a blind eye and hope they never face it. Seeing a group of strangers combat that narrative before my very eyes was one of the most unexpectedly grounding experiences in my little life. It was moving to be blindsided by raw humanity. People expressed their imperfections without fear of judgment or even hope for resolution.

The next morning, we prepared to leave within the solitude of our tents: folding dirt-stained T-shirts, clapping mud-packed tennis shoes, collecting various newfound trinkets, and tightly organizing them into our backpacks to begin the long venture home. The sun leaked through the acacia trees and vervet monkeys leapt from trunk to branch. The coffee was warm and bitter. As we all huddled around the vehicle, the conversation pooled much like all the previous mornings. Although each of us walks a different path in a different place, and we may or may not ever meet one another again, I did know one thing with certainty: We all would leave this place holding on to a piece of each other for just a little bit longer.

give and give some more

even though i gave you everything, i'd dig a little deeper to offer
you all the rest of me

floating in the past

swimming in my memories
dwelling on every word he said to me
i'm drowning with my head above the water

cycles

Letting people go from your life is just as

important as welcoming people into your life.

anxious

*i feel like a deer running in the woods with bullets flying over me
sprinting aimlessly towards an exit nearly caught by a pair of headlights*

but they always miss me, and i keep moving

Chapter Thirteen

Buzzkill

I have to go tonight. I can't back out of another friend's invite to "just please come over . . . it'll be fun!" My chest instantly comes alive like a hill of ants collapsed beneath a heavy boot. I can't cancel. I shouldn't not go. I won't be that guy. But, oh my fucking god, every fiber of my being DESPERATELY wants to be.

Think of clinical anxiety disorder as a lively wasp nest suspended effortlessly from the oak tree branch outside your living room window. It's there. You see it in the center—the swarm of yellow jackets orbiting their paper home. Instinctually, you might shiver slightly at the thought of getting too close. But, on the other hand, your neighbors know nothing of its dangerous whereabouts. They stroll over to drop off a piece of misplaced mail or venture down for dinner one evening blissfully unaware they're feet away from thousands of VENOMOUS GOLDEN BUTTS one false move away from ATTACK MODE!

This is anxiety. A hazard hidden in plain sight. It only affects those who see it. It's only real to those who feel it.

My eyes dart away from my work, onto the clock, and back to my work again in a vigorous cycle. The sun is falling and Friday night is knocking. "I. don't. want. to. go," I sigh heavily to myself. My stomach continues to tighten into knots. "Just show up. Get dressed. Catch an Uber. Say a few hellos and be home before midnight. It's not hard. You can do the bare minimum. What could go wrong?" I role-play over and over in my head as the clock continues to tick, and time moves at an undesired pace.

Everyone experiences nervousness or apprehension, but not everyone knows what it feels like to be physically resistant to accomplishing certain tasks purely due to a level of unexplainable dread that attaches itself to them. For me, one of those is meeting with groups of people. It doesn't have to be a particularly massive accumulation of bodies to trigger these feelings either. I've experienced this at weddings, intimate apartment parties, black-tie galas, patio dinners, friendly game nights, you name it. When anxiety strikes, the setting hardly matters. The rational becomes irrational. My normal flips to abnormal. So, typically, I avoid it at all costs. I predict the future based on history. Which, for someone who craves a more fruitful social life, is not a good habit to have. Do you WANT to die alone, Connor?? NO. NO, YOU DO NOT. Well then get your ass out the door and over to Rebecca's tapas night and ask her girlfriend about her new job, or else your tombstone will say "Here lies a shell of a human being no one ever had the chance to meet because he hid away in his house like a fucking pale CAVE GOBLIN." Those are my actual words of affirmation in case you were wondering.

Cold water hits my face. A cup of minty liquid swirls in my mouth. Dollops of goop rustle their way through my hair. My room looks like a war zone. A recent explosion showered my bed in monochromatic clothing, and even hurtled a pair of socks across the room. Honestly, I'm not sure why this happens every time I get dressed to see other people. I'm very well aware nobody actually cares what you're wearing or what you look like on a night out, but for some reason we spend hours debating the contrary. I can barely tell you what year I graduated from high school, let alone what Dillon wore to the club six weeks ago. Hell, what did I have for breakfast yesterday? BEATS ME. You're going to be in a dimly lit room fighting blurry vision from one too many vodka sodas at best. It's not worth pulling your hair out over a pair of black or blue jeans. Breathe. We're all equally forgettable. I pull on the pair of black trousers, tuck in a white tee, and iron the wrinkles out of a black-sleeved button-up shirt. Perfectly standard. Not overly effortful and not "who invited the slob?" If I'm lucky, I'll blend into a shadowy corner and everyone will think I'm a decorative floor lamp. It's chilling how ideal that sounds.

The knots are tighter now and I'm getting butterflies again. Questions begin pouring into my brain just before I'm ready to call a car and make my way uptown. Who's going to be there? How many people will I know? What if I'm underdressed? Was this a pity invite? Will they be surprised I actually showed up? What if I trip and fall off his balcony and die a horrific death? MAYBE I SHOULD INTENTIONALLY DO THAT JUST TO END THESE PATHETIC HYPOTHETICALS. FUCK. ME. These might sound like minor, irrational thoughts because, well, they are! They're totally nonsensical and shouldn't be a big deal. But that's where this disorder thrives. It lives to stir your insides like a stew and toss in chaotic spices every time you look away. She's a sour bitch and I'd love to push her in front of a school bus. The mind steeps in the questions with no answers. I cannot control this. I cannot predict it either. This soon-to-be forgotten party exists in a vacuum, so why am I so focused on absolving it of unspoken sins? Good things can happen, you know. You aren't cursed.

The Uber ride is brief and uneventful (although the driver did nearly kill us or a pedestrian six times, but that's to be expected). I enter the apartment code (#1463) and make my way up the stairs to the third floor. I'm sweating, but not from the climb. The nerves have now manifested themselves in visual discomfort. "That Le Labo perfume better not let me down. I refuse to be sticky TONIGHT," I murmur aloud to myself like a fucking maniac. I'm passing different doors looking for my friend's and I hear the music from behind it getting louder as I approach. Well, I'm here. So, I'm going to take a deep breath, exhale my (many) demons, try my best to not be a stressed-out buzzkill, and just have a good time!!

Although I frequently muster up the courage to jump into the unknown, it's a toss-up on whether or not it works out. There are ways to ease anxiety and I am finding approaches to better cope with it, but it's situational and heavily dependent upon years of practice. Think of it like a Rubik's Cube: complicated and complex, but ultimately it's solvable. You may not get it the first time. Hell, you may not get it the first one hundred tries. I've grappled for years with the questions: Is this something I will have to accept and live with forever? Or can I conquer my saboteur? Can I embrace these feelings and let them flow through me creating some strange sense of harmony? Is my view of anxiety the problem and not the actual anxiety itself? What if I were to start seeing this as a tiny facet of who I am and nothing more? It's not surprising when I feel it. There is no shock when I meet it. This experience becomes a sign along the freeway, but not a roadblock in the middle of my path. What if I drive my anxiety like the "70 MPH SPEED LIMIT" signs I see every day on the 101? They keep me in check, but they never hold me back.

The room is packed with a few dozen energetic bodies. My friend (and host) greets me with a hug, drink, and invitation to let loose. After he drifts back to the masses, I spot a few familiar faces and my body subliminally moves toward them like metal to a magnet. My heart is pounding, and yes, I am still sweating. Over the blaring pop music people are yelling about where they've been and what they've been up to. It's all as expected. Things are existing as I could have predicted.

We spend more time building barricades for moments that may never occur. Or, at least, I have grown to do it more and more as I get older. The collection of experiences you garner and gather along your life's journey unknowingly carry various weights into your future. I can't go skiing because last time my friend broke his femur and I can't afford six months of healing right now. I'll never tell that guy I like him because last time I did that, the guy I told said he wasn't interested. There's no way I could go on a road trip alone this weekend because last time I never left the cabin. The past doesn't dictate the future is just as true as your anxiety shouldn't tyrannize your present. You always holster the power, whether you decide to wield it or not.

The party music faded behind me just as quickly as it faded toward me. My second car of the night dropped me in front of my dark home just before midnight. I was barely buzzed from the alcohol, but I was energized by another successful fight against my own self. I'd walked with my anxiety, but I hadn't allowed it to lead me, which left a little smile on my face up until the moment I fell asleep.

Oh, and weeks later, I definitely couldn't tell you what anyone else was wearing, nor did it ever even matter.

perfect things

I get so caught up in saying the perfect thing that I

end up not saying anything at all.

limbo

My head's stuck in tomorrow and sometimes I

forget how to show up for today.

france

chests rise and sink
we breathe together
under a humble glow
our souls dance
beside our tongues
in a universe
of our very own
we fall into the night
hitting play again
in the morning

denim sky

honeycomb
and lemon lime
kiss me
i'm yours
buzzcut boy
under the denim sky

Chapter Fourteen

Floating, Feeling, Fading, Falling

L ove is difficult to put into words, but I'll try my best to do it some justice. Where do I even begin? I'm afraid of it after feeling it. Terrified, really. It was the most overwhelming warmth you've ever felt. My body was alive. Arms buzzing like bees in a hive. Stomach turning like a washing machine. Eyes focused like a magnifying glass, yet murky like steam fog rising from a lake. It makes no sense and complete sense at the same time. Love is bright, explosive, violent, and the most important thing to you in the entire world. When you find it, you'll do anything to hold on to it.

Years ago, I was in the madness of it all. Like, head over heels. This was the type of love I'd always longed for, but never knew actually existed. The feelings you get are that of fiction. We could sit in a quiet room wrapped around each other and be perfectly content for hours. Days, even. I used to fly around the world just to see him. "I'm going to Rome on a road trip. Meet me there?" he'd ask as if that were a normal request. "Just booked my ticket," I'd respond without a thought. It wasn't an option. It was the only thing. The things I'd do and the distances I'd travel purely to smell his head and have him nap in my arms. We couldn't be physically close enough. Ever.

"I'm heading home to Australia," he whispered on a four-hour phone call.

"Well, then, so am I," I'd, again, respond with zero hesitation.

I was obsessed with the madness of it all. Chaos followed us in a wake like chemtrails. Drifting through time without a care in the world or any regard to what it meant to live a normal life. Hotels were our home away from home. Our clothes were tossed over lamps and small wooden corner tables. We busted down doors after violently kissing each other through long hallways smelling of cigarettes and minty soaps. We laughed about that a lot—the fact that we enabled ourselves to live a false reality. Black cars, international flights, Styrofoam takeaways, and long showers after fast days. My first love was fiction, and after it was over, I never thought I'd feel that way ever again.

I eventually found the courage to try.

Dating blows. It's ungodly difficult especially in our modern times. Creating a profile on multiple dating apps sucks the life out of me like the Death Eaters in *The Prisoner of Azkaban*. Slurps my pride right out of me like the last noodle in a damn bowl of ramen. Riddle me this: How is a person supposed to realistically depict themselves to another person with five photos, three broad facts, and one concise bio? HOW? DON'T WORRY, I'LL WAIT. Latin would be easier to learn. Hell, I'd rather write an obituary than describe myself in 140 words or less. I'm exhausted before I even begin. I mean, the number of options we have tends to consume our every thought, and surely we'll find a way to pick them all apart.

"I simply cannot like a guy who says his favorite song is vaguely jazz."

"Five photos and you're wearing a hat and sunglasses in all of them? What are you hiding, John from Highland Park? Who are you really?!"

"This man really thinks he's impressing people by only listing all the people he wouldn't date in his bio. No fats, no fems? NO, YOU SCUM."

For the record, I'd like to further reiterate how exhausted I am. The options are endless. Truly. Whatever or whoever you're looking for is out there, but I think we frequently forget the obstacles and losses it will take to find that person. Let's be real, you can find your one-in-a-billion match. But how far are you willing to go to locate them? There is always the chance someone better exists, but are you willing to ruin what you have now for potential? It's complicated. Every boyfriend I've ever had was met online, which is weird even to me now. Our connection was made through a series of 0s and 1s. Digital infatuation.

Collin was a curveball. I'd known him in real life, but we were slowly passing vehicles. A wave and a sarcastic remark were frequently exchanged with little eye contact and infrequent afterthoughts. Then I saw him on an app and eventually we were kissing on my sofa after a few heavy pours of red wine. I'm a slut after dark, what can I say? Collin was sharp. Opinionated, yet funny. After that night, we were nearly inseparable for a string of eight weeks. I vividly remember saying to him at 1 a.m. as I waved good-bye from the sidewalk, "See you tomorrow, I'm sure. Day, what is it, six now?" It was easy to find a way to see him. We had mutual friends and a near identical schedule (meaning we had none because Hollywood, babyyyy!). Mario Kart with his roommates one night, and dinner with our friend downtown the other. I liked him. A lot. But, truth be told, I ran away before I could love him. Taking credit where credit is due: Self-sabotage was our final demise. Ah, I know her well. She's practically family! Like a racist aunt, she's the car crash you can't look away from over Thanksgiving dinner.

I quickly found Collin's "flaws" and didn't allow myself to go any further with him, so I stopped coming over. Those eight weeks occurred like a forest fire and fizzled away like a candle covered up. I still feel bad about that one because I know it wasn't clear why things ended so abruptly.

Noah was a breath of fresh air. We also met online. Crush at first swipe. Gross, I hate that I wrote that (giggling and smiling as I type this). He was nice. So fucking genuine. A real sweetheart. Like a golden retriever in human form. We met up for dinner at a place I picked out. The atmosphere was light, and the food was moderately priced (a rarity in Los Angeles). He told me about growing up a few hours south of here and how he'd dreamt of being a designer. From *Dior and I* to *The September Issue*, I interjected zealously with some of my favorite documentaries about clothing and fashion. A blanket of comfort fell over the table and nerves seemed to fade away. We held hands walking down the sidewalk. One night, he took me in his car to an overlook of the city and played his favorite music. Our faces were lit by the glow from city lights. Our bodies were warmed by each other. What I liked most about Noah was that he respected me. No boundaries were crossed. He was never over-sexual with me (something I'm very anxious about). There was never a moment where he inserted himself into parts of my life that were deemed inappropriate. Much like I did to Collin, I backed away too soon and let Noah down easy. He said he understood, but honestly, I wish he had fought me on it. I was beginning to think I was the problem, not them.

After many flings and a few one-night stands, there was Ben. He was the smartest person I'd ever met. Literally, a genius. A quirky guy flourishing behind a pretty typical life. Again, we met online. His accolades intimidated me, but we met for coffee despite a cold sweat of hesitation. He was much quieter than other guys I'd dated. Reserved. Timid, but in an endearing way. He didn't have to say much, even though I very well knew he could. There was a humility about not oversharing, and holding your cards close to your chest. I fell for him slowly, but hard all at the same time. Like the time in between day and night. One day, I skipped into my therapist's office and nearly yelled, "I THINK I'M IN LOVE AGAIN AND I'M FUCKING TERRIFIED." It was overwhelming. The potential to love again. A thawing of a frost. Relief after weathering a storm. I hadn't thought it was possible for me to love again, yet here I was.

My body was buzzing once again. Ben was in school, but always made time for me. I'd pick him up after a lecture and we'd race to a museum or a hike. He always led with my opinion. Letting me step on a platform and boast my truth. We'd get drunk with my friends and kiss in the Uber ride home. I'd ask what he wanted and he'd say "whatever you do," which made me smile. Our moments alone were sensual and we cared deeply for each other. We started a relationship, and ended it almost as quickly. It happened again. The self-defeating thought. I began to pick apart a perfectly imperfect person and began to only see the things he would never be. The person I wished he was, and therefore, who he actually was was someone I shouldn't be with. Truth be told, like a monotonous storyline, we weren't given a fighting chance to turn into something. Relationships change. They develop like a complex flavor. In time, love becomes something new. I ended it before it even began. They say "All is fair in love and war," but I wasn't to him. He deserved so much better than how we left it.

I'm not a perfect person. I house many impurities and harbor an overhead of baggage. What I say isn't always what I mean. My actions don't always reflect my true desires. Feelings frequently cloud better judgment, and emotions obstruct completely acceptable pathways. What sucks is that I know that. It's clear as day. My defenses are up when they don't need to be, but I can't help but throw a fist just in case. I yearn to love again. I miss that sweet, sadistic, psychopathic cycle. The floating, the feeling, the fading, the falling. Every inch of it. It's all worth it even if it ends.

hope in disguise

i don't know what i want
or who i'm looking for
but my heart wakes with desire
to no longer be so alone

someone new

i need someone new to love me just like i once loved you

old habits

you're bad for me and i know it's true
but my brain is drowning in old thoughts of you

you

you want to be kissed
you want to be loved
you want to be missed
but above all of this
the quiet desire
simply to be thought of
stands on its toes
in a sea of cloudy bliss

Chapter Fifteen

Driveway

E very morning around 7 a.m., my alarm sounds and I get out of bed. I stretch, I sigh, I wash my face, sigh some more, stumble my way into the kitchen to brew a pitcher of coffee, and sit down in front of my computer for a few hours before I muster up the stamina to dip out the door for a run. This routine happens six days a week. Sometimes seven if I'm feeling spicy. But rarely does the pattern falter. Call me a creature of habit or a version of Bret Easton Ellis's American Psycho, but either way, it is how it is. Having a semi-solidified way to begin the day has become a way to set the remaining hours up for certain success. I'm up early, and post-exercise I feel as though I've conquered a small nation before many have even put their teeth into a slice of toast.

When I exit my house, although there are many running routes at my disposal, my go-to begins by taking a right and heading straight down the street for miles on end. The good ol' out and back.

Standard and straightforward. And if I kept running long enough, I'd find myself into the middle of the Pacific Ocean, which is pretty cool. Along this path, the many times I've taken it, I began to notice something strange. The first mile into the run, I cross a busy Los Angeles street and relax into a residential neighborhood. One, two, three homes pass by and I come upon an oddly run-down residence. There's a wide driveway (not usually afforded to homes in West Hollywood) that could fit roughly two sets of two cars parked in tandem within its cracked paved way. The home, or at least I think it's a home, has a wooden canopy stretching out front of its rectangular structure. As I zoom by time after time, one day it dawns on me that there's always a man propped up in the back right corner. He's an older man. Maybe sixties, seventies even. Hard to say, really. He has dark skin and is wearing a black uniform of sorts. A security guard maybe? Some sort of parking patrol? That's odd. It's not an apartment complex and doesn't appear to be a business. Too small. To be frank, its dodgy exterior makes me think no one even lives in it. The windows are dark and the leaves are piling up. But the man, he's sitting there like he's working. Guarding something, even. Hmm, strange.

The routine continues as always.

Wake up, sleepy eyes, wash face, coffee, wider eyes, running. And, yet again, the man is always at his post sitting in a black folding chair under the chipped paint canopy. With no cars around him, he's hardly hiding in that large driveway. If it's a bit cloudy, he can sink into the shadows a bit, but I always notice him without fail. We never wave. He doesn't make eye contact with me really, either. What could he be doing? Even if he's working, who is he doing it for? For many runs, my mind becomes fixated on his potential story and looks forward to catching a new glimpse.

Maybe this is some disguised, chic West Coast recording studio where all the world's most talented musicians go to create their newest hit? Maybe this is a drug dealer's headquarters camouflaged onto a normal street in an attempt to keep their products safe? Maybe that isn't a uniform and he's a homeless man who's found a shady spot to relax under during these desert days' warm sun. Hell, maybe he's just a guy and I should mind my own god damn business. Any of these could be possible. The latter should be implied, but alas, I'm a nosy little twink. That being said, it's difficult to know anything of substance when I only catch a five-second glimpse every morning. Ten seconds if I remember to peek on my way back. And, when all morning I have the exact same portrayal, nothing new is learned or gathered after seeing the same scene over and over again. The gentleman is always in the same position, wearing the same clothing, sitting on the same chair, and looking calmly straight ahead . . . the same. Never a difference. Like, the most realistic marble statue I've ever laid my eyes on. Eat your heart out, Michelangelo!

My routine continues and the calendar pages flip by. This dance keeps twirling and nothing new ever occurs. I, inevitably, reach the point where I lose interest in the stranger, and forget to check if he's there any longer. He becomes a small dent in a white wall that eventually turns near invisible to the naked eye. As I've noticed him, I do wonder from time to time if he's noticed me too. Sometimes I forget that it takes two people to stare at each other. If my eyes find him, his can surely find mine. But I continue on and nothing changes.

Although I've said my routine rarely shifts, it does sometimes.

If there's an early meeting I may run even earlier. If I'm caught up in a stroke of creative work, I may run a bit later. The strange thing is: That man is almost always there. The other morning, I had to catch a twilight flight, so I jogged around 7 a.m., and much to my surprise, the man was there. A few weeks later, I went for an evening walk to stretch my legs after a long day, and he was there again. It seems as though this man never leaves his post, although he must. He's not sleeping there. I see no pillows!! The more I saw him, the more I almost felt frustration toward him. WHO ARE YOU? WHY ARE YOU THERE? WHAT IS GOING ON? AM I A PART OF SOME ELABORATE EARLY 2000s PRANK SHOW, or worse, IN MY OWN VERSION OF *THE TRUMAN SHOW*? If this is all the work of some futurist video gamer, I need you to know: I'M ON TO YOU, ASSHOLES! I don't need answers, but I'd really like some. The longer I wait, the more hesitant I become to approach this stranger. Because again, this is someone I don't actually know anything about. For all I do know, the answer is so simple and unsatisfying. But the many what-ifs keep my curiosity fed and coming back for more like a bowl of food for a stray cat. And my timid Midwestern manners keep me running by with no new answers. Maybe I'll work up the courage tomorrow. Or maybe, I'll mind my own business!

There's something charming about not knowing the truth. Have you ever watched seasons of an incredible television show and put off watching the last episode for days, weeks, months even? The ending so easily obtainable, but you don't want it to be over yet. Whether it be a fear it won't live up to years of expectations or prolonging a story you simply aren't prepared to leave behind. However good or bad the conclusion may be, you're not ready to move on. That's kind of how this feels. After over a year of encounters—yes it's been that! long! now!—what if I've built this mystery up to be something it isn't? What a waste of my imagination. What if the answer isn't as thrilling as the problem itself? What a letdown. As much as this man has no real weight on my life, there has been something exciting and exhilarating to imagining the world he lives in every morning I set out for my run. Even on the toughest workouts, I know my attention can always fall on the stranger stationed in front of that particular structure. A new clue, a new idea, a new chance to expose the wild truth that lies behind him. It could be everything I've pondered over or something wildly different.

One day, I realized: The man was no longer there. For how long, I'm not even sure. I guess I really had blocked him out after seeing him so frequently. He'd become almost invisible over time. It's been months now, so I don't think he's coming back. That home is much stiller now. Resting lonely on the road with all the others. Who was he? Where is he now? It's strange the impact one stranger in passing can have on another. The lives we lead. The secrets we hide. I dwell on that more now when passing people out for a walk or squeezing behind someone in an aisle at the supermarket or talking to an operator over the phone. Each with a story I'll never know, but may daydream about for even just a second. Life left to an imagination can bear never-ending fruit. My mind wanders as I tie my shoes to head back out the door.

Chapter Sixteen

Act Natural

The wind was howling loudly outside like something out of a 1960s horror film, but it was almost unnoticeable inside our wooden cabin resting on some farmland of the Welsh countryside. A group of friends on a little road trip to bring in the springtime. How cute. How quaint. Harry warmed a kettle over the kitchen stove as he sifted through his backpack, spelunking from a brown paper bag at the bottom. He pulled it out and happily began directing the mushrooms within it onto a rugged chopping block. I'm pretty sure he saw himself as a decorated French chef, and honestly, I would fully back up that depiction and award him a Michelin star if I had any right to do so.

"Boys, gather round!" he yelled in excitement. "Who's having what again? Quarter for you? Just an eighth for you? Did you really want a half?? You sure? All right." Mumbling as his eyes panned the room.

The shrooms had now been divided up and steeped appropriately in a gray liquid.

"Okay! Bottoms up!" we exclaimed in unison. And there began the trip.

I'm not one to take drugs regularly, but I'm also not one to shy away from a new experience during a good time. Marijuana? Gladly. LSD? Give me a minute. The older I get, the more appealing these socially taboo encounters seem to become. It definitely boils down to the age-old "if you tell me I can't do something, now I want to do it ten times more" scenario. Now, that's not to say I have a desire to eat CRACK for breakfast or do seven WHIP ITS in the McDonald's parking lot. Give me a little more credit than that. You know I'm practically a cherry blossom with a pulse. But for substances that statistically won't permanently damage me and the ones that I know have come from a credible source, ladies, I don't see the harm in living the little ol' thing called life.

When I was growing up, my dad made a sort of pact with me and each of my siblings. If I recall this correctly, we were told at a young age, "If you don't do drugs, drink alcohol, or get into any major trouble with the law while you're in high school, your mom and I will fund a trip of your choice after you graduate." These trips had rules and guidelines, naturally, but the idea of a big getaway to celebrate being a model young adult seemed like cake to me. Fine. Easy. Done. Kind of an ingenious move there, Dad. A bit funny that we get to go on a trip because we didn't go on a trip, but I like your style and think you're a pretty cool guy.

Anyhoo, as far as I know, we all kept to this agreement (unless there's a liar amongst the four of us . . . doubtful, but I like the plot twist potential) and we all received our promised reward. I decided to backpack around Australia with my first, longtime friend—hostels, kangaroos, the great barrier reef, giant spiders . . . the works! The moment we boarded the eighteen-hour international flight to Sydney, we ordered ourselves both a beer and a glass of wine as fresh-faced eighteen-year-olds. Oopsie? Sorry, Dad. Let's not mention me blacking out from too many shots of cheap corner store vodka my first night at college a few months later . . . or most weekends for the two years that followed. Oh, or the time I jumped through a window and proceeded to sprint like a vegetarian out of a slaughter away from a sounder of police, and finished the night by puking off the top bunk and onto the carpet of my freshman dorm room. There's no time for that here. Stop asking. It's a secret.

Anyways, BACK TO DRUGS—they fascinate me, but luckily, they do not control me—I'm a lucky one in that way, that's for sure. After playing the role of the "good boy" for far too long, I made the active decision to audition for the part of "moderate man" for the time being. As someone who literally went to school underneath a church for eight years, no one has ever in their right mind referred to me as a bad guy. So, in the middle is where I'll settle, right next to the guy who is too afraid to kiss on the first date.

There's something satiating about doing the wrong thing or the thing you've always been told you should never do. Like, the idea of popping an edible right now instead of writing has me TICKLED. Don't do drugs or you'll ruin your life. Don't quit your job because it's too risky right now. Don't get a tattoo because you'll always regret it when you're older. Don't move away when things are perfectly fine at home. Don't push through the pain, otherwise you'll get injured. Don't take the shot if the room's already spinning. NOBODY'S ASKING YOU TO BE A HERO. Being a pioneer is dangerous.

I think it's only human nature to be curious. Hell, curiosity stimulates all the progression the universe has to offer. It's the only real reason we've ever managed to move forward in this world. Someone, somewhere, sometime said, "I'm sick of doing it this way. What if we did it that way!" They challenged the status quo, they pushed past a social norm, and took a leap of faith into the unknown. Oh wow, I must be on drugs writing this. We're just talking about swallowing some funky mushrooms a teenager in an alleyway pawned off on your friend, calm down, GANDHI.

The liquid had been swelling in our bellies for over twenty minutes now, and the effects began to show themselves. The otherwise dull room was illuminated in vivid color schemes. The proportions of its many objects were completely out of whack. The ceiling appeared to be thirty feet high and the hallway must have been the length of a football field. What. The. Fuck. Is. Happening. We all started giggling as if laughing gas had poured into the space. Seemingly uninteresting details, like the vacuum tucked into the cabinet, became a topic of conversation for what felts like hours. "Oh my god. Your red shirt is EXACTLY the same color as those red curtains. Shit. That's amazing," I said in utter disbelief, falling into its daze and utterly infatuated with the similarities. Comically stupid. The whole scene has me in tears simply recounting it.

We continued on being transfixed by our new world's countless details. In the kitchen, someone began performing an improvised version of Netflix's *Chef's Table* with a tray of ice and various vegetables from the store. A bunch of loons, I actually can't believe it. The night simmered down as we babbled on about nonsense and came back into our bodies after floating above them for a solid three hours. The colors came back to normal, and we were in fact still just chewing on ice cubes.

liquid dreams

Perpetual happiness is a liquid in the pipe dream

through every human experience, and we need to

learn how to ride the waves rather than

resist them. Just be.

hold on to it

Find what brings you joy and grab hold of it. Tightly.

fight for it, and preserve it as long as you can.

Chapter Seventeen

Moments After a Fiery Combustion

It's funny, I used to be so afraid to be alone. Not full-on phobia, but somewhere between my time at college and my time in Los Angeles I became uncomfortable in my own company. It wasn't that I had to be with friends per se, but I needed people around me to keep the loneliness at bay—to keep me away from myself. But I don't want to write about those feelings. I want to write about the liberation that comes with appreciating your own company. It's precious and frightening, but worth the investment.

Moments of solitude tend to follow some of life's biggest decisions. If you're accepted into a college upstate or you move across the country for a new job or break up with a partner or your best friend gets married— whatever it may be, moments of peak change are often followed by a blanket of solitude. You've left one "normal" and moved into a new one.

Within a matter of months in 2014, I altered my career path, came out of the closet, broke up with my boyfriend, and moved into a new house.

Talk about an identity crisis. That series of self-inflicted wounds left me writhing in pain and not recognizing the face reflected in the mirror.

Who even am I without all of those things around me? Who am I without him? What am I without them? Can I be better? Will I be different? What the fuck have I done? Did I just ruin everything?

It felt like my life, the one I had been happily building up for years, was now being blown to smithereens, and I couldn't do anything to smother the remaining inferno. There was no normal anymore. Everything was an open wound. And if one more person told me "time heals all," I was going to fucking kill myself. Literally.

Like most things, to better a skill, one must practice. And that applies to the expertise of your own self as well. After that hurricane rolled through my life (you can read all about it in my last book, *Note to Self*), and the storms subsided years later, I realized how important and defining that period of solitude was for me. It's a total cliché, so prepare to roll your eyes, but I wouldn't change any of it even if by some magical act it were possible.

As painful and destructive as that time of emotional turbulence was, the process had become necessary for me to locate my lost identity: who I was, and who I actually am, without a collection of safety nets placed all around me. The new me. The real me. The me I never knew I hadn't already become. A foundation built from the past me for the future me.

When left to your own devices and preoccupied with your own company, your choices, habits, decisions, beliefs, likes, and distastes all come into question. From the breakfast you have to the movie you adore to the way you talk, everything is in sudden madness. "Who. Am. I." This question echoes throughout your cranium from the moment your eyes open to the second they shut (and even haunts you in your dreams if you're especially neurotic like I can be). To become yourself, you must confront yourself. To live a truth, you have to debunk some lies.

Who. Am. I.

The path toward self-discovery was not immediately noticeable at the time. Hell, I didn't ruin my life, look in the mirror, and shout phrases of excitement toward a hypothetical journey I wanted to begin. There was no cinematic turning point where I wept in a mirror and said, "This all stops here. Tomorrow, I change for the better." Reality ain't that pretty, honey . . . Well, to be fair, there was a lot of disturbing mirror weeping, but none of it would be seen as particularly . . . inspirational. It was all quite pathetic actually. Oof. I'm picturing it right now. Gross. Stop this madness. Somebody time travel and slap me across the face. I'm begging you.

The most important step toward change is being open to it. It was uncomfortable to sit in silence and not distract myself from my own thoughts. It wasn't enjoyable to go to dinner alone or to a movie without someone else. What would I order? What would I see? Having a newfound ownership of all the minutes in my day was exhausting until it wasn't. Like any new skill, though, the second attempt is always easier than the first. You practice taking ownership of your life. You rehearse being an individual until it feels natural. You push and persevere. Until, you just are—like the sun rising in the morning; it's a slow-growing light that suddenly bursts the early hours to life. You exist as you are like there's no other way but this. Not better, but new.

Fear once came to me in the form of my own shadow, but I see it less and less nowadays. The window is open, and light pools in the living room. An end unmasks as a beginning.

perpetual

Even in the end, it remained a beginning in disguise.

sounds

drowning back in yesterday
floored by flooding feelings
times have changed, babe
and surely people have too
help me i'm drifting away
into the sounds of my youth

perspectives

Just because it could always be worse,

doesn't mean it isn't bad.

Chapter Eighteen

Pearls

Night is cast over my car like the pre-chorus to a sappy pop song. I'm alone. Rain is falling, which is fitting. And I just broke a heart for the first time in a long time.

Things had been rocky between my former boyfriend and myself for quite some time, but it doesn't make it any easier. A while back, I quickly began to have those dreaded "I simply cannot see a future with you in it" feelings no one wants to have in a relationship. They blow. Hard. Those emotions only cause waves of pain to whirl around them, and are no joy to their host or receiver. And, for me at least, they're like an itch that must be scratched. It's almost impossible to ignore them or hope they evaporate into thin air.

I pull out of the meter parking at his downtown apartment, and at a red light, I dial my best friend to force her to listen to me cry on the drive home. She's in London at the moment, so this bitch better be prepared to accept the international data charges coming her way. My pain is her pain, right? We've definitely taken some version of a marital vow during our six years of knowing each other.

The dial tone buzzes loudly over my speakers. I must have been blaring music on the way over to crush his soul, but had forgotten about it as I was trying to find the right words to say.

Ring . . . Ring . . .

"Babeee! Hey!" Her words somehow sound like a smile.

"I did it. I broke up with him. He was so shocked. I'm a horrible person." I cut her off sharply with tears already bubbling around my eyelashes.

"Oh, no. Connor. I'm so sorry. You must feel horrible, but you're far from a horrible person. You knew this had to happen. Some people have those feelings and keep relationships going for years! What good does that do for anyone? It may not seem like it right now, but what you did was an act of kindness to you both." She lets this out with ease as if she's a trained psychiatrist.

She's not wrong and she echoes something I already know deep down. This had to be done. It's not fair to string a person along and treat them like a puppet. I had a boy do that to me for years, and I swore I'd never put anyone else through the wringer like that. False hope is cruel. Like presenting a slice of cake to a dog with no intention of allowing him a taste.

"I know you're right, but . . . I don't know. He was just so broken by it. It was horrible. And . . . I don't know. I feel like here I am, yet again, one step away from being happy again. Things don't have to be easy, but do they always have to be this hard?" My words stumble out through various sighs and wet-mouth noises. Gross.

"Listen, the one thing I won't let you do is put yourself down here." Oh, now she's cutting me off. "You're a catch! Anyone would be lucky to have you! Look. at. that. ass. COME ON."

I giggle, but my face quickly falls back into my palms.

"It's going to be okay. I know you'll be fine. And, remember, you have me! I'm here for you tonight, tomorrow, and then some!"

God, she's good. She knows exactly the words you need to hear. Other times, she's a vile little shit bag, but I digress. Friendship is a vital. It's a rare resource, but when found in its purest form, it'll fuel your vehicle for a lifetime.

I've been searching for friends my whole life. The desire to fit in closely with a group of people has been an eternal struggle. I'd always get jealous of other kids who had a clear best friend. Ride or die. Their one and only. I'd get close, but continually fall short of first place. There's nothing worse than being a third wheel to two eternal partners. After a while, it loses its appeal, like eating plain oatmeal when there's a jar of sugar on the table.

With each new chapter of life comes a new opportunity to find people to share it with. In middle school, I joined the swim team and encountered five of the weirdest people I'd ever met. Naturally, we quickly became inseparable. Seventeen years later, I've been in three of their weddings and expect to be in the other two as well. After endless days of fart jokes, bags of Sour Patch Kids, countless midnight movie showings, we all drifted our separate ways to college. Connected to this day, but beginning a whole new journey of friendship. At college, I made more friends. Some stuck around, others dwindled away as our individual lives increased in complexity. I moved to Los Angeles soon after and continued the search.

I think what people miss with modern friendship is how rocky it can be. The older you get, the more isolated you can become. You don't have a school to attend and naturally create random encounters. People are increasingly working from home or for small corporations, so there's little chance to see new faces there as well. Not to mention in 2021. There's a little lady called Miss Corona Virus drifting through every neighborhood in the world. She's silent but deadly, and makes conversing with strangers near impossible. It's hard to talk to someone through a mask from six feet away without generating fear or mild panic. Not necessarily the greatest recipe for lifelong companionship.

Looking for friends as an adult is frightening and deeply vulnerable. You have to open yourself up to awkward encounters, lengthy backstories, sweaty yoga classes, sexually tense pottery courses, oh my! Okay, those sound kind of fun (really fun . . . ugh, I'm becoming my parents), but what I'm trying to get at is it's infinitely dissimilar to being thirteen and meeting a cool dude in science class who you see every single day for four years. Connection in adulthood takes mutual effort and patience. Two things most of us are running low on as it is. I'm exhausted and unhinged! How dare you ask me to be otherwise! *hiss*

what's a life without a little sin

placed myself in a cage
and let the calendar flip by
losing control of a life
that has always been mine
defeated, disillusioned, derailed
my body burst into flames
tripping over street cracks
falling victim to self-blame
really, it's a pure shame
things got as bad as they did
what's a life without a little sin
brightening, bursting, blooming
catapulted towards a better me
melted into a marmalade
flying above a sea of evergreen
if existence is heavenly
cut the pleasantries
open the gates
watch me run

bodies

this body makes me feel far too much
i fixate on its shape and its taste
racing towards a different waist
it's a spiral, a drunken obsession
only lost time appears on a scale

i often wonder what it's like to worry less about my flesh
a forever companion to fathom and mind
the only thing in your possession from birth until death
and yet, we fight tooth and nail to alter it daily
picking and pulling it apart
cutting and sewing into a fresh start
my mirror destroys and rebuilds me in minutes

i've been bad, i can't have that
we've been good, we deserve it
this cycle of justification
i may not love it all the time
but it's mine
and only mine
so i will learn to live inside it

Chapter Nineteen

Easy As It Goes

I finally feel like I've got a grip on most aspects of my life. For now, at the time of typing this, that is. And, not to throw that in there as a mild sedative or looming foreshadow, but simply as an acknowledgment to the ebbs and flows of reality. From nearly twenty years of personal experience, I know these kinds of things come and go in unpredictable waves. Kind of like a weather pattern: It's possible to see a storm coming, but it's impossible to predict the exact second of daybreak trailing the clouds. One day you're on top of it all, the next year your world is all lubed up and you couldn't stand on two feet for more than two seconds even if you tried—a bit gross metaphorically and semi-unnecessary . . . but I hope the picture has been painted! Like I've exclaimed to an exhausting extent prior, I tend to forget to write about the good periods life brings, and you know what? These really have been some gosh darn genuinely good times! GOSH DARN, I SAY! Sitting here just off of Melrose Avenue, coddled in the smells of espresso and blueberry almond scones, I'm giving myself permission to bask in the extended bright slice of time I've found myself in for months now. This isn't rare, although my inner saboteur screams the contrary, and I know it. This existence is a sweet peach and today is sunny, baby. Roll on over and have a taste. I'm ready to highlight my efforts, glowing growth, and all the unforeseen triumphs.

If you don't already know, I'm going to let you in on a not-so-secret secret about me: I'm a fucking emotional mess of a human being. My feelings bear the strength of steel or diamond or Captain America's biceps, and sometimes I don't know how to properly handle or compartmentalize them. This is my truth, hear my sobs! Being diagnosed with depression back in 2016 (or 2015? I can't quite remember because I was DEPRESSED) was oddly the beginning of a slow, strenuous, uphill climb back to normality, and unknowingly, to new levels of robust willpower. I didn't realize how far gone I was at the time, but shit . . . I had fully lost myself to the clutches of that crippling illness.

You know when you look back at old photos you used to take of yourself as a teenager and cringingly exclaim, "Uh, I . . . simply do not know that person nor do I associate with anything they ever did or said!!" It's a similar type of feeling. Well, kind of.

Rereading old journal entries, tearing through old photo albums, and generally thinking back on those days, I'm met with a level of disassociated disconnection. There's a layer of fog that coats those years, and I'm not fully sure how I was able to escape it. How exactly did I find the daybreak that accompanies the storm? Could have been the medication I took. Could have been the endless therapy sessions I attended. Could have been levels of perseverance and resilience I somehow have within me. Could have been pure chance and luck that brought me back to stability. Honestly, it feels like a cocktail of it all topped with a screwer of who-the-fuck-knows, but regardless I'm here. I've made it back and I for the first time in a while have something I'm afraid to lose: my own life.

Backing out of these sad words, I'm here. I'M HERE! The other side of the tunnel is bright, bitch! It's so funny to now be on the far side of the mountain, where the air is soaked in potential. These days are like experiencing some level of mythical magic because I forgot what it felt like to not dread a normal day. I forgot what it was like to exist freely without constant anxiety and dread. I forgot, but now I remember.

modern humanity

how lucky are we
to breathe in a century
where love knows no limit
a pool of human difference
so deep you can swim in it
the potential of her
almost anything can occur

mirroring accolades of him
exists as you are
to live is no longer to sin

friendly

Pain befriends open ears and embracing hearts.

Chapter Twenty

Lucky Stars

Often I get caught up in reflecting on how fortunate I am to experience a sliver of difference in my existence. The last seven years felt like a rebirth of sorts. My eyes opened to a vibrantly diverse world, and once I saw it, they could never close again. I dove deep into dark water, and found silver at the bottom.

Ever since moving away from home—and really, the only world I ever knew—a new reality confronted me, one that had never even crossed my mind. It sounds so strange to type this, but when you've unknowingly been locked away in a monochromatic bubble, it's shocking to escape and see color. Literally. My entire high school was composed 99.9 percent of students who looked exactly like me. We walked in hallways filled with mirrors. We ate lunch amongst mannequins. And we returned home to neighbors lacking any nuance. A sea of white, modest, religious bodies floating in a pond no one dared to disturb. Rarely new, almost always the same. And that's fine . . . until you learn it's not.

Growing up, I cannot think of a time I was confronted with diversity in any sense of the word. From religion to race to gender to sexuality—we rarely encountered anyone who didn't fit the mold. It's almost painful to think about now. Things would have been so much different if that weren't the case. The new perspective, horizons, experiences, conversations, lifestyles, stories . . . the list could go on for miles. It's like looking up close at a white canvas painted only with thousands of cream-colored lines. When you slowly step back to see the artwork in full view, inching farther and farther away from it, the strokes begin to melt into one another, and soon all you see is one cream-colored canvas. But, if the piece had strokes of red, dashes of emerald and eggplant and granite, no matter how far away you were from it, you could still make out those unique colors.

From seeing the world to meeting new people to discovering myself, I thank my lucky stars I was able to see the dashes of color blossom all around me.

lost all my better days

i always forget to write about the better days
because in those moments i'm surrounded by such immense joy
that words I sketch into paper cannot do justice
to the electricity happiness emits
but i will try my best to express it

Chapter Twenty-One

Loud Sounds and Where They Come From

The more I hear certain idioms, the less meaning they hold. Listen, you can tell me you only live once or life is short, don't let it pass you by, or quit wasting all your precious time, or some other cliché wood-sign-in-your-mother's-kitchen bullshit. But that doesn't mean it will actually do anything to me. In fact, it may just infuriate me. You, a kind soul, may have the entirely opposite outcome you were attempting to have here. Fruity quotes seem to do less and less for me the older I get.

Nowadays, I'm reminded of my humanity when I'm not even looking for it. Moments that unexpectedly ground me in this reality: a gust of wind on a quiet night or ripples of rain on a still body of water. Mundane days can be met with a bolt of electricity that brings me to tears or makes me dance in euphoria.

Days can feel repetitive or eerily familiar. Especially during a certain global pandemic I'd rather not write about right now because it consumes every other moment of my twenty-eighth year on planet Earth. Aside from that spooky trauma, a typical day passes by its melancholy in a blink, leaving me wondering what I actually accomplished.

"What did you get up to this week?" my sister asks over the phone.

"Um, uh." Pausing with confusion. "I'm not sure. Not much, I guess. Just the same old, same old." I give the most vanilla answer humanly possible. BUT THAT'S JUST HOW IT REALLY IS SOMETIMES. Sometimes, nothing goes on. There is not a single thing that is up. What is this, a courtroom? Stop interrogating me, JUDGE JUDY. Life is repetitive by nature until someone's tossed a wrench in the gears.

Loss becomes a more common occurrence the older you get, unfortunately. There is no bright side to it; I reject anyone who spins it that way. Someone's lost life belittled to "a part of a greater plan" is offensive to me. But I can't help but notice there's a continued side effect of losing a human life in your orbit, and that's a wake-up call. When something awful occurs, you're inevitably reminded of how porcelain human life truly is. Our bodies feel resilient, and they may be to a limited extent, but accidents do happen. Tragedy strikes blindly.

The heart of a girl I grew up with stopped out of nowhere while she was walking into work last year. She was twenty-seven. A friend I made from my early years on YouTube fell victim to a drunk driver earlier this year on the night of his birthday. He was twenty-five. I hate that it takes pain to remind me of joy, but it does sometimes.

Loss is never fair. What happened to Erin and Corey should not happen to anyone. Yet, here we are. Reduced to a memory. What happens next? The feelings that follow grief are a punch bowl at a frat party. Devastation, enlightenment, clarity, melancholy, etc. I tend to allow myself to crumble like a Nature Valley granola bar, and swiftly make my way to the "where the actual hell can I go from here" phase. It's stretching after a long workout—annoying but important.

Death rings oddly of life, so every person I love receives a multitude of calls and messages sounding my appreciation for them. I'm overcome with the value friends and family bring to my daily life. My dad calling me on his way home from work to talk about his patients and the weather. My friend sending me a photo of a hot boy we both can gush and lust over. My brother FaceTiming me just so I can watch my niece crawling around the room squeaking 'pup pup!' at their three-year-old dog. My group chat talking shit about some random person or raving about a stupid meme we're all in tears over. These are daily occurrences that rarely receive loud, boisterous applause. The patterns we weave ourselves into cause us to momentarily overlook how special and valuable these facets of our routine are to forgettable weeks. Luckily, it's not only horrible things that seem to ground me.

After spending more time on my own, I've begun to open my ears to more small, quiet moments that shock me out of a dull cycle. Picture a zombie. Any one of them. A *Walking Dead* zombie. A *Scooby-Doo* zombie. A toilet-paper Halloween-party zombie. Whichever you want! Now picture them fast-walking down the sidewalk at 6 p.m. like a grandma who just got a Fitbit for her birthday. That's me! Every evening! I'm a fast-fast-walking Fitbit grandma zombie.

Nearly every night nowadays, I pull on my shoes, set my house alarm, and dip out to get some fresh air before dinner. Recently, I've also been leaving my phone at home to truly free myself of any distractions. This is how I force myself to appreciate life itself.

The air is cooler now, and it smells like autumn even though it's January as I'm writing this. Cars honk on a busy street to my left and kids are giggling behind a fence just up ahead. Everything is green. Like, truly vibrant green. Life envelops the grass, and the lemon trees line the pavement. A hummingbird zooms by and pauses mid-air searching for another beaming flower to borrow a sip of nectar from. People are switching on their living room lamps as the sunset prepares her exit. Their bay windows glow tangerine from my view on the purple streets below. The days are getting longer now. We're making our way to spring. The connective energy marinates in melodrama despite the perpetual summer we live in. It's all very predictable now.

We're living in tandem with the chaos these days and searching for hints of normality. All the seemingly unimportant details from the walk I take every single night somehow bring a blanket of peace to my mind. Even the ones that occur time and time again. These moments are loud. They echo into the neighborhood. I'm awake to them and their scents of sudden joy. I'm brought back to earth and feel human yet again, so I turn around and make my way back home.

This practice gets pretty hippy dippy ippy—even for me—an agnostic Virgo with a few crystals and buds of weed stashed in his bedside table. I have no hesitation in admitting they help me find a sliver of stability in the especially manic world we live in. They remind me that I'm just one person trying my best to walk through the dark and only stumbling a few times. As far as we know, this remains true: You only live once, and life is short. It's easy to get caught up in the hustle adulthood demands of us: the project deadlines, presentation preparation, making dinner for your family, remembering everyone's birthday and locating the appropriate gift to give them, the endless chores, the constant laundry, calling your mom, paying your debts, writing a speech for an old friend's wedding, attending another's funeral. We do so much for so many, and that should not go unseen or underappreciated. But do not lose yourself to your calendar, or waste your thoughts on tasks that don't really matter. It's hard to be human, but that doesn't mean it isn't an honor. You don't have to be alive for every moment of every day, but do take the time to soak in soft and loud sounds. They're all around us. Can you hear them?

thawing

i see spring in the morning
there's a thawing in my head
my eyes begin warming
reflections follow a thread
clarity takes her needle
and i'll continue growing
again and again and again

a turning point

You left me. You lied to me. Over and over again.

You ruined me and acted like it was normal. I lost

my innocence. My happiness. You took everything.

Maybe the world may never know exactly

what you did to me. What you took from me.

But I'm done caring. I'm done with you and this me

I never asked to be.

flesh and bones

You are more than the body you inhabit.

Flesh may be temporary, but what it creates

is forever.

on the right path

A major step toward acceptance is acknowledging

its existence.

Chapter Twenty-Two

Hidden in Plain Sight

I sprinted toward where the ocean met the sky—a fine line drawn between the Earth and the Heavens. My pulse jumped, beating rapidly. My feet followed that speed in tandem. Racing. Running. Everything I had cared about moments ago melted away as I fell into the blues beyond me.

"I AM THE EMBODIMENT OF HUMAN RESILIENCE!"

I screamed into the void.

"THIS MOMENT IS MY ONLY DEFINITION!"

The words left my lungs at full capacity.

Seawater soaked into the off-white canvas around my feet. Waves crashed ahead, and mist dusted my body like stars in a winter sky. Even drugs would have found jealousy in the current state of my mind.

"I AM LIMITLESS!"

My voice projected into infinity.

"THE FUTURE I WANT IS MINE FOR THE TAKING!"

Self-gratitude welled up in my throat and within my eyes. This was a life worth living. I was a person worth being. Worthy does not begin to describe the respect ignited within a soul that for so long felt everything else. I staggered to a stop and looked out toward the gradient of color falling before my very eyes.

"I'm here. This is it and there is nothing else," I said, almost laughing in this the madness.

And, without hesitation, I continued my propulsion onward with no end in sight.

fortune-teller

*

i see infinity at least twice a day
a man on a bench
parked with the morning paper
kids by the ocean
sand flies as they spring to the water
it's a perfect melody
a well-orchestrated dance
everything exists in harmony
and, I keep moving forward

cosmos and madness

It's not a question of who put us me here or

why . . . it's about living a whole life regardless of

the reason. A limitless existence. A dip into the

cosmos. Not to work yourself into a grave or to

wake up already wishing it were tomorrow. No.

Fulfill your very own definition of purpose as you

fall deeper and deeper into reality's mania. Every

waking moment blooms with saturation if you're

open to seeing God in the mirror.

red

i'm passionate
and furious
i'm a heart near explosion
i'm dancing
and delirious
i'm every essence of human emotion

searching for harmony

to live fully for today you must disparage yesterday's
problems and disregard tomorrow's possibilities
this moment is your most valuable belonging

Chapter Twenty-Three

A Higher Power

I wish I had the imagination to believe in God. And, yes, I know that sounds severely condescending. Apologies. What I mean to say is: In my current state of mind, I find it next to impossible to conjure some blind faith in the existence of an almighty, higher power who intended for all the world's suffering, inequality, and injustice to occur. I will admit though: Wishing for something greater than this finite reality does whisper of blissful wonders into my ears. That cannot be denied. Believing in something far beyond our blip of an existence is mightily delicious; again, I will wholeheartedly admit. But alas, my hope has dried up like a lemon forgotten in the fruit bowl for so many complicated reasons. That's not to say I'm hopeless by any means though. Actually, with time, the thought of an eighty- to one-hundred-year expiration date sounds some shade of poetic! Like a perfectly executed film with ribbon wrapped around its closing scene where all your questions are given answers or fade away softly into insignificance. Let's go there. I want to explain these thoughts more. Here's a look through this age-old religion kaleidoscope with bright eyes and a benevolent heart.

Being a Midwestern boy who went to church every single Sunday—my family and I even went when we were out of town, or even the country (we once went to an absurdly humid religious service on the island of St. John during a summer holiday)—and since I'm someone who attended a small Catholic school and all-boys private university, you'd think those teachings, values, morals, and practices would have trickled their way into the remainder of my life. However, you'd be wildly wrong. Don't be presumptuous. It's rude.

Growing up nestled within the rolling hills of a chilly lower corner of Minnesota, my parents always put in the effort to take me and my three siblings to church, and, I cannot stress this enough, I was always bored out of my absolute motherfucking mind. Check his pulse, the electrocardiogram is suddenly showing a flat line. The far-too-complex concept of faith never quite hooked me, so during my adolescent years, it didn't frighten me to not believe in a God or an effervescent afterlife, because well frankly, it seemed fictional. Can you really be afraid of something that doesn't even exist? What surely did send a shiver straight down my sedentary spine, though, was the mere thought of my parents finding out I'd never in all my years had an ounce of heavenly faith in me. There's nothing worse than hearing the fatal words "we are very disappointed in you." Stab me in the heart slowly, I'd rather go painfully. All right, well, apart from when my own self-interest came into play in the form of, say, the desire for a holiday-gifted Nintendo 64 or a gleaming "A" on the exam I hadn't prepared for, or even the miraculous transformation of my youthful gay ass into a youthful straight ass—then I'd be praying morning, noon, and night. Which, specifically regarding the homo latter option, is laughably ironic. Consider, in theory: I'm asking THE all-knowing creator of the entire fucking universe to change his/her/their always-accurate creation into something other than what he/she/they already planned for. Oh to be young and wish you weren't GAY. How naive. You won't get the video game system, Connor, but you will enjoy remaining queer, just you wait and see. Nevertheless, I exclusively used religion to my adolescent benefit, and when I didn't need it, honey, I didn't want any part of it. Kinda messed up. As they say: out of sight, out of mind. Ignore the problem and it will simply disappear, right? But, oh boy, did those sixty minutes every Sunday morning feel like a waste of my precious limited time. I'd rather be watching Cartoon Network. Sue me.

As I grew older, I increasingly became more resentful of specifically the forced participation organized religion appeared to require. There was something about venturing to the same location at the same time with the same people reciting the same words in an overwhelmingly mindless, unanimous manner every single week like clockwork that made me feel . . . icky. The whole routine felt so ICKY! What more can I say?

In fifth grade, one portion of our education's curriculum was dedicated to the memorization of the books of the Bible. The task was simple: be able to verbally recite all sixty-six names listed in both the New and Old Testaments, and *drumroll*, you pass! *Donezo! Perfecto! Fín Achevé!* My personal choice of method to obtain said triumphant end result was forming a catchy rhythm to the names that made up the Bible's books; a prolific Gospel banger, if you will. Lady

Gaga, before "Judas" (2011), if you will. After days of remembering, reciting, and rehearsing, I walked out of that one-on-one oral examination on the third floor of St. Peter's Catholic School with a perfect score of 66/66. Ha! Score one for TEAM JESUS. Blow me, Satan!

Putting the achievement aside, to this day, there is something about the act of mindless memorization and recitation that I haven't been able to shake. I shit you not, I can still get through half of those biblical headers, and I haven't attended a church service by my own free will in a decade. A DECADE. Genesis, Exodus, Leviticus, Numbers, Deuteronomy . . . Hello, 911? I'd like to report a case of chronic brainwashing? Those names were implanted in my underdeveloped preteen frontal cortex and have somehow burrowed their way into that ludicrous space forevermore. Or, at least for now. Dementia runs in the family. Who's to say any of this will stick with me longterm *cold sweats*. In the meantime, pay rent, you Anno Domini freeloaders! My hard drive space up there is nearly at capacity and I need all sixty-six of those square nanometers back!

Just before I aged up to the *Encyclopedia Britannica* definition of an adult, I remained in attendance of weekly mass purely to please my parents, but being the sly snake that I was, on occasion I would "go to a different service at a later time all on my own because I liked the priest more." And those, readers, were some of the only times I blatantly spit a boldfaced lie in my parents' direction, and if my horrendously parked 1998 Honda CRV had been struck down by a lightning bolt in the middle of a sunny summer of 2010, it wouldn't have shocked me. To be fair, I did like that priest more, but that's like enjoying eating a giant bowl of unsweetened, cold oatmeal because you hid a single raspberry somewhere within it.

Later that same summer, however, I did genuinely go to a different service at the crème de la crème, the holy hometown pièce de résistance, the massive cathedral in downtown La Crosse, Wisconsin. While naturally arriving late and hiding my shamed self in the far back pew, I began to lose interest around about minute six. At that point, my 2009 Blackberry Storm may have popped out of my pocket and magically into my hand with the Facebook app (it was a different time, hold your judgment, foul paper flipper) open and fully functional. And, in a quick stroke of fate, as if maniacally planned by the big boss upstairs thyself, the case-less cellular device slipped from my hand and onto the stone-cold flooring—echoing shame throughout the mass attendance, shattering its glass, and only further proving to me that "I don't belong here!!!" and now I'm clearly uninvited by the host as well! Karma's kiss from her chapped, wintered lips.

I know it may not be right, but being the (fully embraced) gay son, I've been allowed certain privileges. One of them being: I'm fully okay to break out of familial norms and able to carve a brand-spanking-new path that ultimately is unlike that of my siblings. I'm unsure how I was awarded this unspoken opportunity, but its existence is undeniable. Just ask my siblings: They won't deny it, and yes, it is subtly annoying to them too. Say hello to my three tattoos and counting! Religion most definitely falls under this rainbow umbrella. My parents are very much aware I no longer have any attachment to religion, and knowing how much the practice means to them, I continue to question how this "lifestyle" (we'll ironically call it that) goes unnoticed and unbothered. But it does. It's not like I expect them to force their views upon their twenty-eight-year-old son, but I am surprised there is no longer any active pushback. Maybe it's quiet disappointment? ANYTHING BUT THAT. Maybe it's not and I'm waking a sleeping Christian bear? OH, DRAMA. Nowadays when I venture home for a birthday, holiday, or semi-frequent parental surprise, the invitation to attend a church service is extended, but typically turned down due to "jet lag" or "work that needs doing," which isn't fully a lie or fully the truth either. It's become a very "you do you and I'll do me" topic, and really, I'm not certain there's more that needs discovering there. For the time being, I'll let that 350-pound grizzly slumber.

Believing in God does sound divine. It really does. I have moments of wishing I could UNO Reverse my thought process and live despite this enlightenment. Religion provides community, values, clarity, and a destination with a reason to not go absolutely batshit crazy over the thought of a dark mortality void that we're all slowly and willingly walking toward. MORE COLD SWEATS, AM I RIGHT? So, having that unshakable belief in your life and afterlife seems outright special. If it isn't hurting other human beings, it seems completely all right as well.

Sitting here typing my way through this thought process, it's hard to articulate exactly why I can't believe in more. Like a French crêpe cake, at a glance there are too many layers to easily decipher how many and what flavors they really contain. I think it all stems from the notion that I'm not confident. I even want to believe in something more. If that point held validity, I feel like it would be so messed up. Over three billion humans live in poverty in 2020. Seven hundred and ninety-five million people in the world do not have enough food to lead a healthy life. Chronic diseases are responsible for 60 percent of global deaths. Countless people die suddenly from unexpected accidents and are swept away from their loved ones. Hatred, prejudice, and bigotry run rampant throughout modern society. If you're a female, LGBTQIA+, or BIPOC, you're disadvantaged without question. The world can be so cruel and so cold. It's hard to have faith in it most days. If all of this is all a part of a great plan masterminded by some mighty deity in the sky, well, then personally speaking here: I'm not sure my conscience could rest easy supporting and uplifting it. It feels wrong. And, like, if I'm incorrect about a heavenly existence, will I seemingly be struck down in some horrific way? Or, alternatively, will I burn in a fiery pit for all eternity? Despite all the good I've done and try to do every single day? That doesn't rest easy with me. It's Gaslighting 101. I'm in a maze with only dead ends and no exit. Fear alone should cause me to believe, but it doesn't and I can't fully explain why. Even if I am wrong, it has all still been worth it, you know? Once I opened the door of doubt that led toward these epiphanies, I could not go back to close it no matter how hard I try. The odds are equal here. I very well know I could be wrong. It's why the older I get, the less I joke about God and the more I accept we're all humans simply trying our best to leave the planet overflowing with hope, fulfillment, and peace. If you believe in God, don't let me sway or discourage you. The best part about the heavenly conundrum is that there is no definitive answer, so we can all get along in knowing nobody knows anything for certain. It would be too easy if we could see our inevitable fate and know exactly what's behind the emerald-colored curtain. Where's the fun in faith if we deem the meaning obsolete? I'd love for everyone to understand that more—that there are billions of people in this world in search of similar outcomes, but all with individual methods.

As long as your beliefs and your actions affect others in the world around you in a positive manner, the rest falls to fate. Build yourself, and those around you, up. Always. To the beyond and even higher. Toward something better than all our bests. Peaceful religion isn't a waste of time, and bold atheism doesn't befriend nihilism. It's complex and so are we, so give yourself to the enjoyment that comes with curiosity. Question everything like a child for the first time in a contemporary art museum. There is plenty of good that can come from us all if we all agree to open ourselves to a conversation with the cosmos. I believe in that.

i believe in today

To belittle someone else into your own beliefs is a

gamble on the truth no one can ever know. I'd rather

place my bet on this exact moment. The only real

thing you can ever be sure of is here and now.

Chapter Twenty-Four

Pushing Up Daisies

My feet were kicked up and I was lounging in one of the turquoise Adirondack armchairs out back on the deck at my parents' home late in the afternoon. It was summer and the air was thick with humidity. In spite of it, with a chilled IPA at my side and a freshly cracked book on my lap, I welcomed peace with open, moist arms. After a few hours taking in my childhood backyard surroundings, my dad, arriving home from work dressed in full medically appropriate garb, opened the door to join me in the oasis. Dr. Franta is a curious, intelligent, but silly man with seemingly endless amounts of energetic drive pulsing through his veins. Even after a long day at the clinic, he somehow manages to magically pull a few more Jenga blocks out of his tower, only stopping just as it's about to tip over (into bed and start the process all over again). I've always admired that about my dad. He's a doer. A pursuer. A "go go go" kind of guy with rest nowhere on his radar. Someone who rarely complains about tasks that need completing and, in a strange way, is almost looking to add more to his overflowing plate, even when it's just been set onto the dinner table. Oh, and he can fall into full-blown REM sleep anytime, anywhere, and I think that's pretty fucking rad too. I can't relate, but it's a cool talent nonetheless. After settling himself into the beach-themed seat next to mine and general small-talk having subsided—How was work? How far did you run? What's for supper again?—he, in his typical tangential nature wonder, spits out of nowhere, "So, what do you think happens when we pass? Like, after we . . . die?" aloud to me. Dropping my book below my eye line with my interest piqued, I reply, "Well that's out of the blue and pretty morbid considering our paradise setting. Did something happen at work or is this just one of those random thought-provoking questions?" He was quick to push it on me, simply curious at where my mind would go, and why I would define such a conclusion. Typical. I delightfully indulge him.

This is the way I like to see it. There are four very popular paths to take into consideration here: science, science fiction, religion, and the ever more popular "there's no possible way to know this, so why bother talking about it" approach. Now, the last one is a bit on the nose, so let's focus on the remaining three options.

Roughly 13.8 billion years ago, the rapid expansion of matter from a state of extremely high density and temperature marked the origin of the universe as we know under the title "the Big Bang." This was the only time we know of in which something came from nothing. Our entire blueprint to existence popped into actuality seemingly out of thin air. Well, no, that doesn't even properly apply here because there was no air. "Nothing" is a difficult concept to imagine, but I think you understand the concept here. So, how is that even possible? How is that not a ridiculous act of pure fantasy? Alexander Vilenkin, a cosmologist at Tufts University, recently said, "The way the universe gets around that problem is that gravitational energy is negative." That's a mathematically proven fact. So, with the energy of matter itself being positive, and the energy of gravitation being negative, that means together they combine to a sweetly satisfying cocktail of zero. Aka, nothing. Therefore, this "does not violate any conservation laws" says Vilenkin. Radical, right? I love it.

Let's meditate on that for a moment: It may be possible for something to come from nothing. That is an outlandish thought, which to me makes it all the more thrilling. I love learning something nonsensical is actually very sensical. It flips my perspective; alters the norms preprogrammed into my brain. Suddenly, I begin to apply it to other aspects outside its realms. Hearing something like this only broadens my horizons and makes me open to the fact that: Anything is possible. Were there once dinosaurs stomping around this lush area of land I now refer to as my parents' backyard? Hell yes, there were! Sure! Why not? Sounds like a party! Is it possible that there are human spirits floating around the crusty antique store that's been down on Main Street since 1950? No doubt! Of course! Why not? Could there very easily be more than two genders to the human experience? Signs point to yes again! It's actually already been proven! Gender is a social construct! Again I'll scream, WHY NOT? Each of these, however scientific or fictional, is very much possible! If something can come from nothing billions of years ago, and we can comprehend it this very second, then shouldn't we question everything we've ever been taught—even if just for fun? No surprise, but it's a yes from me!

At this point you may be thinking, "Who knew I picked up a philosopher's guide to astronomy textbook from Barnes & Noble this afternoon? Get to the point or I'm returning this false advertisement, sir!" Okay, all right. Take a deep breath and hold your horses. (By the way, did you know that phrase comes from the 1600s? When someone broke the law, they were tied down to a piece of wood, laid on the ground, then a group of held horses would be released to trample the criminal. CUTE! Anyways, I'm doing it again, I know. Back in we go.)

Death according to science, although almost magical at times, is pretty straightforward. When we die, that's it. Lights out. Boom. Done. The End. Thanos snap. Game over. We either decompose in an expensive box under the earth or get burned into flakes in a glorified artisanal wood-fired pizza oven. Now, nobody likes the sound of that one. It's a bit bleak, and a difficult reality to swallow. That's why more uplifting theories have remained at the peak of societal popularity.

According to the book of Genesis in the Christian Bible, the world and first-ever human being were created roughly six thousand years ago, before 4000 BCE. Then, soon after, some queen named Eve got a little peckish one morning, sunk her teeth into a little scrumptious red apple, created all original human sin, and ruined everything for everyone forever. Now, that's a power move if I've ever read one. Category is: Girl Boss. Placing historical blame on an independent woman who knew what she wanted and took it from the very beginning? I'd pretend to be shocked, but I'm too busy not being surprised. Anyways, Mary-Joseph-the birth of God's only son Jesus-miracles-miracles-oppression-miracles, spook ooky tada, and we're here in the present day. I think most people totally won't be offended by a fourteen-second summary of Christian creation, right? I also think, I don't really care right now.

Anyhoo, according to Revelation 11:12, after people die, they go "to Heaven, wrapped in a cloud . . ." and live where God lives. Well, not live. Reside. I don't think renting an apartment would be a viable option. It's more of an "owning everlasting beachfront real estate" type of thing. Quite the serve, if I'm being honest.

Venturing through my adolescence and into my teens, the idea of dying and going to heaven always sounded lovely to me. Well, aside from the whole "fear attached to messing up and residing in the fiery pits of hell doomed to burn for eternity alongside Satan" ordeal. I did think about that after typing "Naked Men Touching" into Google far too many times. Not gonna lie. However, it was comforting to think if I continued being the good little Christian boy that I was (forget me talking about gay porn two seconds ago), I would, in a way, live forever. No pain. No suffering. Eternal love with all my friends and family. Well, unless they screwed up and ended up in the fiery pits of hell doomed to burn for eternity alongside Satan. I'd hate to be the bearer of the bad news in the afterlife. JOYOUS! The basic morals attached to that religion, and most to be honest, are well intended. Be a good, kind person and everything will be okay for you. Love your neighbor as well as yourself. Honor others and be generous with strangers. I can get behind all that. It's not far off from how I try to live anyways. If you take away the mistranslations, misinterpretations, judgment, wars, exclusion, and general lack of shift with the evolution of our intelligent society . . . maybe it's not so bad! Plus, the idea of a heaven is just as magically bizarre as science telling me nothing came from something. Oh, and speaking of the supernatural . . .

Flash-forward just a few millennia into modern times. The simulation hypothesis or simulation theory is the proposal that all of reality, including the Earth and the rest of the universe, could in fact be an artificial simulation. Although there is no set year this idea was created, it has been popularized during the Information Age of the late twentieth century and only grown since the knowledge of technology has severely exploded. During the dawn of the computer, nerds and kooks alike have become obsessed over the idea that our own reality could be paralleled to the video games your twelve-year-old cousin won't stop playing. Whether it be Super Mario Bros. or Animal Crossing, it doesn't really matter. It all leads us to believe: Everything we know could very well be an illusion. The words you're reading in this book could be a part of your very own illusion. Preferential. Personalized. You are now the owner of your very own illusion. There may be no confident future pathway or definite emotional stability, but a semi-probable digital simulation all to yourself. Wow, congrats! You really did that, girl!

The mere thought that all of this reality could be a part of some sick, twisted celestial gameplay has me shaking like the peach in *Call Me By Your Name* after it read its script for the first time. It's both relieving and revolting. Astounding and annihilating. Somehow spectacular and sinister at the same time. I, for one, would love to know who has my controller up there beyond the stratosphere, and would love even more to tell them to cut it THE FUCK out. Stop MESSING AROUND and FOCUS. I. Am. EXHAUSTED down here. Good lord.

If the simulation theory is accurate, dying isn't really a thing (and potentially living isn't really either), so what happens after all of this isn't really up for discussion either. Well, unless this is level one of a thousand. In which case, I'll need an IV off Casamigos to keep going. Existing is exhausting. That theory begins to cross over with a Buddhist perspective where you live on forever with many different lives. Every time things end, they begin again just as quickly. It's quite the pleasant thought to be honest. That nothing is nothing to fear because you never get a chance to meet it.

When you collect all three of those main routes toward inevitably pushing up daisies, they all make me think of one thing: It's all ridiculous, isn't it? You die either (1) knowing you were alive during the most ideal scientific boom the universe has ever seen, (2) believing your whole life has led you to live on forever with a powerful overlord residing in a utopia just beyond our concept of dimension, (3) hoping some genius had the skill to create a virtual reality so realistic no one ever figured out our lives were all one big human Tetris game and paying taxes or mowing the lawn never actually mattered. It's fucking bananas. Laughable regardless. All major outcomes are kinda mental, aren't they? It makes me think this world we're lucky to reside in is so brilliant because there's so much to still be discovered. We've barely scratched the surface of our own potential. The bounds at which we understand how humanity ticks.

I stopped myself from talking and lowered my face from the now bright pink sky. As I panned over to my dad, he was smiling and relaxed into the monologue I had just given. He took a sip of his soda and raised his chin to the spot mine had just left. "It really is a mystery, isn't it?" My mom's voice called from inside the house, asking if we were ready for dinner, so we made our way inside.

The unknown overpowers the known time and time again. You overturn a stone just to find another stone underneath it. It's magic and madness just the same. Every bit of it. From life to death, no matter the pathway or the outcome. We stare at the fire and find ourselves falling into tomorrow.

peace found a home

I am everything. Even when I feel nothing at all.

everything

Life refuses to be contained. We are a gradient of

moments. A chase of chemicals. A scattering of

experiences. The sun in the trees, bread baking in

the kitchen, crying out of love, silence that follows

pain. Today, you are everything and nothing at all.

Life refuses to be contained.

heaven

to live beneath the red trees
reclined amongst the sunbeams
daydreams with a cool breeze
mint leaves with a grape squeeze
to die amongst the clouds, please
nothing exists beyond me now

humming

just in case we don't live forever
we should probably do it twice
in the event of the inevitable
let's hope it grants us tonight

i plant my feet firmly
into soil that surrounds me
falling less towards temptation
leaning into a voice speaking profoundly
it hums like a bird's wings
sounds sweeter than lilac nectar
they deliver themselves tender
ruminating as doubts fly free
we drift away together

and, i am taken as i am

I'm thankful for it all, really. The pain and the

pleasure. All the quiet joys and the loud despairs.

The rosy peaks and the indigo valleys.

I've been shaped by every second of every minute.

Constructed into a chronicle. Refined by my own autonomy.

Born to never occur again. But, watch me

bleed until the sun sets.

Acknowledgments

The people close to my life make me a better person, and I owe each of them an eternity of gratitude, but let's begin with some tender words of affirmation that may make them a little uncomfortable.

To my editor, Loan: Thank you for ingesting my writing and pushing me to develop its sentiment even further. From my eccentric creative approach to my emotional tiptoeing across all the fine details, you bring grace and care to this book's process every step of the way.

To everyone at Atria publishing: Thank you for continuing to believe in me as an author and aiding my pursuit with this blossoming passion. Your support over the years has left me feeling nothing short of humble and uplifted.

To my designer, Samuel: Thank you for bringing my vibrant vision to life with the cover art. You're a peaceful soul with an electric eye for design, and I appreciate all the thoughts you have to offer.

Acknowledgments

To my team, Andrew, Cait, Clayton, Ryan, and Lindsay: Thank you for all the hard work you do, but more important, thank you for your friendship. This decade has seen sunny afternoons and thundering evenings, but you're always here for me. You stand by my side and that belief and persistence is something I will always love you for.

To my friends: Thank you for bringing excitement and chaos into my life. I can be worried and I can be tense, but when we're together, you never fail to keep me grounded in the moment and thrilled to be alive for today. I fucking love you all to pieces.

To my family: Thank you for always being a constant source of light and joy within my life. You radiate compassion for others and have the ability to make me laugh at the drop of a dime. From the constant calls to the spontaneous trips, I look forward to every second we have together, and I love you with all my heart.

And finally, to you, the readers: Thank you for making what I do both possible and worthwhile. To create is one of the greatest gifts, but to have people care about what you've created, now that is something special. You bring unexplainable meaning and purpose to my days, and I am forever grateful to have the opportunity to share the magic in my mind with the masses. I am happy, and I owe you everything.

About the Author

Connor Franta is an award-winning author, content creator, entre-
preneur, and humanitarian who uses his expansive social media plat-
form to advocate for and spotlight the LGBTQIA+ community. He has
amassed nearly half a billion views on YouTube, garnered more than
20 million followers across his social platforms, and is the CEO of the
companies Common Culture and Heard Well. His public speaking en-
gagements have put him on the same stages as Prince Harry, Naomi
Campbell, and Hillary Clinton while working with brands such as Goo-
gle, Calvin Klein, Target, Samsung, and Nike.